HEART AND MIND

A Synchronous Dance with Higher Dimensions

VERNIECE ROSS

Dear Esteemed Reader,

Thank you immensely for choosing this book to join your collection. We imagine that you've already embarked on an exploration of ideas within these pages, and we couldn't be happier about it!

Now, if you find yourself chuckling, pondering, or even debating with the words in front of you, we'd absolutely love to hear about it. If you can spare a few moments to pen down your thoughts in a review, we would be as delighted as a dictionary on a spelling bee!

An Amazon review would be excellent - but hey, we're far from picky. Whether it's a scribble on the back of a grocery list, a tweet, or even a message in a bottle (though that might take a while to reach us), your feedback is gold.

Writing a review might not be as fun as a spontaneous dance-off, but we promise it'll bring grins to our faces, warmth to our hearts, and incredibly valuable insights to future readers.

With Gratitude,

Verniece Ross

Table of Contents

Introduction

Welcome to a journey of self-discovery and self-mastery, a journey where we'll explore the profound relationship between our thoughts, emotions, and the life we live. This book aims to guide you towards synchronizing your feelings and thoughts with the life of abundance you desire. Be it financial abundance, nurturing relationships, holistic health, or any other form of abundance that resonates with you. This is not merely about 'wanting' or 'wishing' but about aligning your innermost self with the universe's infinite intelligence, steering towards heart-centered living, and utilizing your mind as an artistic tool. It proposes tapping into higher consciousness, embracing the symphony of inner unity, and harnessing your inherent power to manifest a prosperous life. Also, it underscore the importance of being present, techniques to monitor your emotional frequencies, understanding the art of shadow work, and the power of gratitude. Your future is abundant, harmonious, and awaits your claiming, let's begin this journey...

Tapping Into Higher Consciousness and Infinite Intelligence

Now that we've laid the foundation, let's explore the concept of tapping into a higher consciousness and infinite intelligence. This concept is not as abstract as it sounds. In fact, it's as tangible as your next breath. Higher consciousness allows you to access a state of awareness beyond your typical day-to-day thoughts and perceptions. This heightened perception gives you access to a more expansive knowledge and understanding- the infinite intelligence.

Tapping into higher consciousness is akin to shifting your cognitive gear to a higher level where everything becomes much clearer and more lucid. You start to see things differently, understand better, and as a result, you can take more effective actions. It's transformative, opening new possibilities for you to understand and manipulate your reality towards abundance in all facets of life.

But how do we access this seemingly elusive consciousness? How do we synchronize our thoughts, feelings, and emotions to align with the life of abundance we desire? The process is surprisingly simple, and it begins with mindfulness. Being truly present in the moment lets you perceive beyond the ordinary and habitual thoughts that often dominate our minds. By engaging in practices such as meditation, breathwork, and non-judgmental observation of our thoughts, we tune into this exceptional plane of awareness.

Distractions are plentiful in our chaotic world, and mindfulness helps us center our thoughts instead of letting them run rampant. By disciplining the mind, we allow space for a more profound, more potent wisdom to flow through us - infinite intelligence.

Imagine infinite intelligence as a vast ocean of knowledge and understanding that we can tap into at any time. It embodies truths beyond what we know with our limited senses and perceptions. By accessing this incredible resource, we can navigate complex challenges and uncover paths to the abundance we seek.

Also, consider the infinite intelligence as an ever-present guide, a compass leading us on the right path. When we disconnect from the outside noise and align with our higher consciousness, we hear this guide more clearly. This alignment can uncover answers to our deepest questions and solutions to our most perplexing problems. It's like being in a dark room and suddenly finding a switch to a light that illuminates everything.

At this stage, you might be asking yourself, 'Does this mean emptying my mind of all thoughts?'. The answer is no. The goal isn't to clear our mind of thoughts since an entirely 'empty mind' is not possible. Instead, we learn to observe our thoughts objectively without judgment or reaction, thereby developing a calmer and more controlled mindset. The key is not to cleanse the thoughts but to transcend them, to elevate our consciousness beyond the plain of ordinary thinking.

Mastering this higher level of consciousness brings with it a serene calmness, a palpable tranquility that anchors you amidst life's storms. You'll notice a feeling of intense calm and peace, a warm sensation that envelops you. This serenity isn't only psychological but extends to the physical body, bringing about a relaxation, a soothing composure that's the hallmark of mindfulness.

As you become more proficient in accessing higher consciousness, you'll find yourself better able to cope with stress, anxiety, and other negative emotions. Instead of reacting impulsively or emotionally, you'll respond with wisdom and composure. The power to control your emotional responses, to remain stable and peaceful even in the face of adversity, is one of the most significant benefits of this practice.

Moreover, the higher consciousness and infinite intelligence do not exist in a vacuum. They are resources available to everyone without any discrimination. Your educational background, profession, social status cannot stop you from accessing this wealth. What matters is your desire to seek, to tune in, and to harness it.

Accessing your higher consciousness and tapping into the infinite intelligence is a gift that has the power to transform your life, leading you from scarcity to abundance, from confusion to clarity, and from stress to peace. All it calls for is practicing mindfulness, patience, and a persistent pursuit of self-awareness and deeper understanding.

In the forthcoming chapters, we will delve deeper into how we can further unlock this potential - the wisdom of the heart, harness your mind power, achieve inner unity, and generate prosperity. Bear in mind, the journey to high consciousness is less about acquisition, more about unlearning - unlearning behaviors, beliefs, and habits that bind us to lower consciousness. It's a beautifully inward journey that thrills as much it enlightens.

Synchronicity: The Dance of Universe

The magic of life lies in serendipitous moments of alignment, when everything seems to click into place as if the universe itself conspires in your favor. This phenomenon is what we call synchronicity - a concept first forged by famed Swiss psychologist Carl Jung. It highlights how certain events in our lives, devoid of visible causal relationships, yet are meaningfully interconnected. Synchronicity is a beautiful canvas painted by the Universe, blending the often separate aspects of our existence into a cosmic rhythm that's both breathtaking and intriguing.

Imagine experiencing a day when you find an unexpected solution to a long-standing problem, meet a stranger who seems to say exactly what you needed to hear, or stumble upon a book that mirrors your thoughts. All of these could be forms of synchronicity expressing the inherent interconnectedness of the universe. They're signs that you're aligning with the energy of the universe, tuning into its gentle rhythm, and getting ready to dance.

When we start to accept synchronicity as a real and impactful phenomenon, we intensify our relationship with the universe. We're acknowledging the subtle hints, the winks and nods from an energy far greater than our own. It's as if we're playing our part in a cosmic orchestra, contributing our unique notes to create a collective symphony of connected events.

Synchronicity is not just about recognizing these meaningful coincidences; it's also about aligning your consciousness with the ebb and flow of the Universe. It speaks volumes about an individual's evolving consciousness and its rhythmic alignment with the cosmos. It's the universe's friendly reminder that we're not alone, that we're all interconnected, and that our thoughts, emotions, and actions have profound implications in shaping our reality.

Life isn't random chaos. It's a beautifully arranged mosaic of interconnected events, people, and experiences. We call this idea the law of synchronicity, seeing life as an inseparable whole rather than fragmented parts. It's a philosophy grounded on the assumption that every moment holds a purpose, every event has significance, and everything happens for a reason, even if we may not yet understand it.

Our thoughts and emotions play a significant role in inviting synchronicity into our lives. Just like a radio, we can tune ourselves into different frequencies by shifting our thoughts and emotions. Once we align with a higher level of consciousness, we experience a greater frequency of synchronistic events. Simply put, our internal world mimics the dance of the universe, and the universe mirrors our inner dance.

Recognizing this magical harmony and understanding how to create it is a crucial step towards attracting the life of abundance you desire. Often, we're kept at arm's length from our dreams, not because they're out of our reach, but rather because we fail to align with them on a deeper, more intuitive level. We must learn to outfit our inner compass to the magnetic pull of the desires to be aligned with them perfectly.

By being conscious and intentional with our thoughts and emotions, we become co-creators with the universe. The dance we share with the cosmos mirrors the swirling of galaxies far away. Our consciously chosen thoughts send ripples into the universe, influencing the course of events and steering our lives in the direction of our deepest desires.

Yet, while our thoughts matter, the real catalyst in this dance with the Universe is emotion; that raw, potent energy brewing just beneath the surface of our consciousness. Emotions are the songs we play to the

Universe, each one sending out a unique melody that resonates with and draws in matching harmonies from the cosmos.

Emotions are the embodiment of our deepest desires, and they hold immense power. Harness this power, and you hold the key to unlocking a world of synchronistic encounters and abundance. Embrace your emotions, learn from them, and use them as guiding points. They might just lead you to the dance floor where synchronicity comes alive, and the music of the universe guides you.

Learning to tap into synchronicity is a dance in itself. It's a delicate waltz that requires patience, letting go as much as guiding, surrendering as much as steering. It's about feeling the beat, getting in rhythm, and allowing yourself to move with the flow rather than against it. It's an invitation to trust the universe fully, have faith in its complex choreography, and dance with the assurance that you're right where you're meant to be.

Synchronicity is your cue that you're in sync with the Universe and its endless abundance. It's your confirmation that you are dancing to the cosmic rhythm, playing the right notes, and aligning your desires with the Universe's flow. So next time you experience a synchronistic event, give in to the music, move with ease, and enjoy the dance of the universe. You're on the right path, aligning with the abundance that the universe offers.

The universe is always ready to dance with you; are you ready to dance with the universe?

Chapter 1

The Wisdom of Heart

As we delve into the depths of our journey, we encounter an intuitive knowing that often gets overshadowed by the cacophony of the external world: the wisdom of the heart. Deep within us, our hearts pulsate with a potent wisdom, a silent, yet dynamic, intelligence that transcends beyond cognitive processing and rational analysis. This wisdom knows no deceit; it's the quiet whisper in the midst of chaos, the gentle nudge towards our genuine authenticity, and the both palpable and elusive force guiding us to our truest desires and highest potential. Our hearts have the ability to perceive the subtle undercurrents of reality, to discern what's truly vital to us, unswayed by societal expectations or external pressures. Being heart-centered isn't about neglecting logic or brushing aside the intellect; quite the opposite. It's about creating a symbiotic relationship between the heart and the mind, in which both the emotional and rational selves are honored and integrated. Such heart-centered living fuels life with authenticity, enriching it with depth, clarity, and an unwavering sense of purpose. When we learn to heed, harness, and honor the wisdom of our heart, we align ourselves with a natural, intuitive compass, guiding us seamlessly towards the abundance we seek.

Tuning Into the Heart's Wisdom

As we journey through life, there are moments when we need to pause and dig deeper within ourselves to tap into an inherent wisdom that resides within our hearts. This process of leaning into the heart's wisdom is not always easy. It requires vulnerability, courage, and surrender—it requires us to let go of our preconceived notions, our fears, and our doubts and to trust in the guidance of our heart.

The heart's wisdom is inherently intuitive, connected deeply with our bodies, and our emotions. It is a wellspring of understanding that does not rely solely on logic or reason, but rather on feelings and sensations. In some ways, it can feel like an invisible, subtle guide within us, urging us towards our true path and authentic self.

So, how do we tune into our heart's wisdom? Herein lies the beauty and mystery of this transformative journey—a journey that is unique for each one of us. What works for one person may not work for another. Our hearts communicate differently, in ways which are most accessible to us. However, there are a few universal practices that can aid in turning our attention inwards, towards the wisdom within our heart.

Meditation is a powerful tool for tuning into your heart's wisdom. It quiets the chatter of the mind and creates a space of stillness where you can listen to your heart. Some people find that physically placing their hand over their heart during meditation helps them connect more deeply with their heart's wisdom.

Intention setting is another potent practice. Begin by making a sincere intention to listen to your heart's wisdom. An intention can be as simple as a spontaneous heartfelt desire or a purposefully crafted statement such as, "I am open to the wisdom of my heart." By setting an intention, you are signaling to your subconscious that you are genuinely ready to listen, and this readiness creates an opening for your heart's wisdom to arise.

Aside from meditation and intention setting, spending time in nature often brings us closer to our heart's wisdom. Nature has a particular way of touching and awakening our hearts. The quiet beauty, the wide-open spaces, the rhythmic sounds—all these draw us into a deeper connection with ourselves, and thus with our hearts.

Being around people or experiences that elicit strong positive emotions can also be a channel so as to tune into our heart's wisdom. Love, joy, inspiration—these are the language of the heart. When we open ourselves to these powerful emotions, we align ourselves with the heart's frequency.

Of course, tuning into the heart's wisdom is not just about connecting with positive emotions. Our heart's wisdom is also found in moments of emotional discomfort. Hardship and trials often carry powerful lessons that reveal deeper truths about ourselves and our life understanding. The key is not to resist these challenging emotions but to sit with them, embrace them, and see what wisdom they have to offer.

Movement practices such as yoga, tai chi, and dance can also help us tune into our heart's wisdom. These practices engage our body and bring our attention to the present moment. In this space of presence and embodiment, we can listen more deeply to our hearts.

Journaling is another valuable tool for uncovering our heart's wisdom. When doubts or confusing emotions arise, write them down. Let them unfold on the page without judgment or expectation. In this raw, unfiltered process of self-expression, you may be surprised by the wisdom that emerges.

Lastly, trust is an essential element in tuning into your heart's wisdom. Trust in the process, trust in the journey, and most importantly, trust in your heart. Believe that your heart knows what it's doing, and it's guiding you towards the highest expression of yourself.

Remember that tuning into your heart's wisdom is not a one-time event. It's a day-to-day, moment-to-moment practice, a gentle leaning into the whispers of your heart, a continual opening to the wisdom within.

So, here's an invitation for you: Take a deep breath. Honour your courage. And embark on this beautiful adventure of tuning into your heart's wisdom. It may not always be comfortable or easy, but I assure you, it will be rewarding and profoundly transformative.

Heart Centered Living

At the heart of every human, there's a compass guiding us towards the life we desire. But how can we tap into this innate intelligence and profound wisdom? The answer lies in heart-centered living, a harmonious approach that interconnects our thoughts, emotions, and actions with the deepest core of our being.

Heart-centered living isn't merely a philosophy; it's a lifestyle that promotes an innate understanding of our true selves. By leaning into this wisdom, we elevate our consciousness, achieving a life abundant in peace, joy, and fulfillment. It is the honest acceptance of who we are and who we aspire to become. It focuses on the concept that our heart holds an innate wisdom that, once accessed, can lead our lives towards the richness we long for.

Imagine a world where every decision comes from a place of love and compassion, not fear and insecurity. Such a world is possible through heart-centered living. This approach encourages us to confront our fears, embrace our imperfections, and cultivate a deep connection with our inner self.

The journey towards heart-centered living begins with self-awareness. It's about recognizing our emotions, acknowledging our needs and desires, and understanding how they influence our thoughts and behavior. As we deepen our self-awareness, we can learn the language of our heart, using it to navigate the seas of life with grace and wisdom.

Secondly, heart-centered living requires us to cultivate an attitude of self-love and self-kindness. Instead of harshly judging ourselves for perceived shortcomings, we learn to embrace our imperfections and view them as unique aspects of our identity. This loving kindness towards ourselves harvests an environment of internal peace and self-acceptance.

Next, heart-centered living fosters understanding and compassion towards others. It involves empathizing with their struggles, celebrating their successes, and offering our support when they need it. When our hearts are filled with kindness and understanding, our actions uplift not only our lives but also the lives of those around us.

Furthermore, heart-centered living also involves managing our energy. We need to stay attuned to how certain situations, relationships, and environments affect our inner state. By consciously deciding to engage only in circumstances that align with our heart's wisdom and nourishing our energy, we create a path for abundance to flow freely in our lives.

Another vital aspect of heart-centered living is creativity. When we live from our hearts, our innate creativity blossoms. With an alignment towards our true selves, we find unique, creative solutions to our problems, paint our lives with vibrant colors, and find joy in expressing our unique individuality.

The pursuit of heart-centered living offers an invitation to mindfulness. Its practice urges us to stay present and fully engage in each moment, whether it's a simple daily task or an important life event. Being present anchors us to our heart's wisdom, allowing each moment to unveil its pearls of wisdom.

Living a heart-centered life also requires courage. It asks us to explore the uncharted terrains of our heart and to be vulnerable. The courage to undefendedly express our emotions, be it joy or pain, fosters an authentic and genuine connection with our true selves and the people around us.

In the heart-centered living paradigm, every setback is an opportunity for growth. Instead of viewing hardships as obstacles, we can see them as signs that we are out of alignment with our heart's wisdom. They offer valuable insights to realign with our truest desires and our purest self.

Additionally, gratitude plays an integral role in heart-centered living. Gratitude is the heart's way of acknowledging the love and abundance currently present in our lives. It paves the path for joy and happiness, shifting our focus from what's missing in our lives to what's abundant in them.

The undertaking towards heart-centered living is deeply personal yet universal. It's the journey to the deepest corners of our heart, where love, wisdom, and peace reside. It's a path that leads us towards a more intimate understanding of our true selves and sheds the light on the divine connection we are all part of.

In conclusion, heart-centered living is a holistic approach to life that interweaves love, compassion, mindfulness, creativity and courage. It promotes a closer relationship with our authenticity, fostering a life brimming with peace, joy, and abundance.

Chapter 2

Harnessing Your Mind Power

To make the shift from a life of scarcity to one of abundance, we must first understand the tremendous potency of our minds. It's not simply about positive thinking—it's the seamless integration of cognition with emotion, and the realization that your thoughts are the very building blocks of your reality. Just as a potter molds clay, your mind employs thoughts in the co-creative process, shaping your world with every conscious and unconscious idea. Yet remember, the mind is a tool, not the master. Its unbridled power should be tempered with wisdom, pairing logical reasoning with intuitive nudges to glean profound inner truths. Like an artist blending colors on a palette, you're free to entertain, revise, or discard thoughts until they produce the vibrant portrait of life you desire. Investing in this mental mastery is essential, for the journey of heart-centered living that started in the previous chapter gains momentum when bolstered by the disciplined power of your mind.

Using the Mind as a Creative Tool

Imagine for a moment the vast landscape of your mind, a vast expanse seeped with the potential for creating everything you desire in your life. It's much more than just the place where your thoughts and opinions reside - it's a powerful instrument that, when harnessed properly, can lead you on a journey of self-discovery, growth, and remarkable achievement. It's a storied tapestry that can narrate the epic tale of the life you aspire to lead, weaving your dreams into reality.

There's a great truth in the powerful adage, "As a man thinks, so he is." By understanding that your mind is a dynamic and potent foundation for creation, you're essentially tapping into the source of your abundant potential. Using your mind as a creative tool starts with seeing it for what it truly is — a catalyst for positive transformation. Just as an artist uses a chisel to carve a sculpture, your thoughts and beliefs shape the world around you.

The key to effectuating this transformation is to guide your mind to envision and embody the possibilities of the life you desire. This may require quieting the clutter, doubt, and negative chatter within your mind. But remember, you're not attempting to eliminate these entirely, you're just refocusing the lens of your consciousness on your positive intentions and away from unproductive worries.

When working with your mind as a creative tool, it's essential to imagine vividly. Imagine your ultimate life, filled with joy, abundance, and fulfillment. Picturing this in your mind is the equivalent of drawing a blueprint for a building: once the blueprint is completed, the structure can start to be built. Similarly, once you've forged a clear mental image of your desires, the Universe can work to bring it into your reality.

Concurrently, pair your visualization with a strong emotional response. Those who've had significant breakthroughs from using their mind as a creative tool will confirm this fact: the emotional response to a mental image can be the driving force propelling its manifestation. So allow yourself to not just imagine to achieve, but also to feel what it's like to live your dream life.

Another critical aspect of using your mind creatively is sifting through your belief systems. You're a storehouse of beliefs, some of which serve you, while others hinder your progress. Therefore, it's paramount to identify and let go of any limiting beliefs that may act as obstacles in your journey to manifesting abundance.

Mindful affirmations can become a handy tool in programming your creative mind. Frequent repetition of positive statements strengthens the neural pathways in your brain, helping you embrace and embody these affirmations. They're little seeds of potential that you're planting in the fertile soil of your mind—each affirmation nurturing growth and progress in your life.

Furthermore, it's essential to stay open-minded and curious in this journey of exploration. When you're using your mind as a creative tool, it can indeed prompt some unexpected thoughts and ideas. Treat such moments as opportunities to stretch beyond your comfort zone and explore the uncharted terrains of your possibilities.

Remember that your mind doesn't differentiate between reality and imagination, so through visualizations, we are essentially creating a new reality in our thoughts. Time and again, science has shown us that the mental rehearsal of an event creates neural pathways, similar to those created by the actual experience.

To truly harness your mind as a creative tool, it's crucial to imbibe a sense of discipline and consistency. It's beneficial to designate specific periods each day for focusing on your creative mind exercises. This way, you're affording yourself mental space, familiarizing yourself with the inner workings of your mind, and gradually building up the skills required to channel your mind's expansive potentials efficiently.

Lastly, embrace patience in your journey. Just as a tree doesn't bear fruit overnight, the process of shaping your life using your mind as a creative tool too has its own timeline. Manifestations take time and come to fruition at their own pace. You're here to cultivate a sense of comfort in this waiting period, knowing that your desired life is on its way to you.

By viewing your mind as a powerful creative tool and trusting in its inherent potency, you can manifest an abundance of joy, prosperity, and satisfaction in your life. You are intertwining your thoughts, emotions and actions in harmony with your aspirations, creating the perfect symphony of an abundant life. Here's to your journey of co-creation with the Universe!

Thoughts as Building Blocks

Your thoughts serve as the foundational blocks of your reality, bringing form to the previously formless, and influencing how you respond to the world around you. These mental constructs aren't idle, passing elements of your consciousness. Instead, they're dynamic, impactful elements that contain immense potential. Like a skilled sculptor fashioning clay into art, your thoughts mold your life.

Every thought you have is an act of creation. Every idea, whether fleeting or persistent, has the potential to create immense change. In the grand theatre of life, each of them are important players, continually forming and reforming the narrative of your existence. They are not just impressions; they're every color on your palette, every note in your symphony, every word in your life's book.

It's essential to understand that thoughts are energy forms. This isn't some fringe scientific theory but a mainstream quantum physics understanding applied to the mind's functionality. Our brain, mind, and thoughts are constantly transmitting and receiving energetic information. Thoughts aren't simply abstract ideas; they carry a certain vibrational frequency that resonates with the universe.

If you've ever noticed a change in your mood after dwelling on negative thoughts, that's the energy of your thoughts in action. Conversely, positive thoughts carry a different frequency. They instill feelings of happiness, peace, and fulfill a sense of optimism in our lives. When you understand this, you realize the power you hold within you.

You can sculpt your reality with your thoughts, actively attracting the things you desire into your life.

How we think largely drives our feelings, emotions, and ultimately actions. Consistent positive thinking can inspire uplifting emotions, instigate beneficial actions, and foster healthy attitudes. Adopting a mindset of abundance, for instance, results in feelings of gratefulness, contentment, and positivity. This affects your actions, prompting you to take opportunities, be generous, and live life more fully. Your reality starts to mirror your abundant thinking.

The converse is also true. Habits of negative thinking instigate feelings of fear, anxiety, and scarcity. These feelings often lead us to avoid opportunities or act out of fear, further solidifying our negative thoughts. The cycle continues.

Yet, there's a silver lining in this interplay of thought and response. Once you acknowledge your thought patterns' pivotal role in your life, you can consciously shift them towards ones that serve you. And changing your thoughts is like changing the direction of a ship. It might be slow at first, but even a small shift in trajectory can lead you to an entirely different destination.

Acknowledging this power you hold, you might wonder, how can you harness these building blocks effectively? Well, the process is not complex. It just involves paying attention to your thoughts, acknowledging their presence, and steering them toward positivity when you notice any negativity. Positive affirmations, visualization exercises, and mindful living are all tools you can use to direct your thoughts towards your desired reality.

Think of your mind as a fertile garden. Let thoughts of joy, prosperity, love, and wisdom be the seeds you plant in this fertile soil. Water and nurture these seeds every day with shared laughter, acts of kindness, moments of gratitude, and the thrill of discovery. Beware the weeds of fear, anxiety, doubt, and negative self-talk. As you tend to this garden, watch as it blooms into a manifestation of your dreams.

As you explore the power of your thoughts, it's crucial to couple this cognitive shift with heartfelt belief. Without belief, the transformation remains incomplete. You must imbue your thoughts with mindful intent, allowing them to resonate with the beat of your heart, creating the symphony of your existence.

As we delve further into the balance between intuition and logic, remember that thoughts as building blocks are one part of the equation. They work in tandem with your emotional intelligence to shape your experience. However, acknowledging the power your thoughts wield is a critical first step in crafting a life imbued with abundance, fulfillment, and joy.

In essence, pay attention to your thoughts as you would a cherished friend; respond with compassion when they detour into negativity, celebrate when they resonate with positivity, and guide them gently back when they lose their way. Nurture an inner dialogue that supports your aspirations, and in time, you'll see your thoughts manifest your desired reality.

The Balance Between Intuition and Logic

As we continue down our path of personal growth focused on harnessing the powers of the mind, we need to recognize an essential balance, namely the marriage between intuition and logic. Too frequently, we view these as two separate components of the mind, with one often dominating the other. However, they can and should function synchronously to create a harmonious cognitive balance that will better help us shape our realities.

Your intuition might be seen as a hunch, a gut feeling, or an inexplicable knowledge that guides your decision-making process. It operates on a preverbal level and often holds wisdom beyond your conscious mind's grasp. Sometimes this wisdom is overlooked as we allow logical thinking to overshadow these subtle nudges.

On the other hand, logic represents our ability to reason, categorize, measure, and align our thoughts with what we know. It provides a basis for our actions and decisions upon what we have learned and experienced. Undeniably, it's an invaluable tool in navigating the complexities of our world. Yet, when we over-emphasize on logic, we might neglect the gut feelings and hunches, which are crucial inputs from our intuition.

The issue here is not to figure out which is right and which is wrong or to even decipher which is superior. They both are vital for a balanced life. Instead, the goal is to achieve an optimal blend of intuition and logic. This is not about taking sides, but about unifying two normally opposed forces to leverage their individual strengths. How might one achieve this elusive balance, you may ask?

Begin by paying close attention to your intuition, quieting your mind to listen to that internal voice. Realize that intuition is not some mystical, nebulous concept. It is a real, discernible aspect of our cognition. Psychologists and neuroscientists are finding more and more proof of intuition's legitimacy and effectiveness all the time. When a hunch or feeling surfaces, don't dismiss it out; instead, consider it as valid and valuable as a logical conclusion derived from evidence and reasoning.

However, don't let intuition steer your course entirely. Implement verification processes through the use of logic. Crosscheck intuitive pulls with logical reasoning and analysis. Is your intuition in line with facts and rational thought, or does it contradict them? Sometimes, you might discover that intolerable contradiction between the two. In such cases, it could be worthwhile to dig deeper and seek additional information.

Yet again, neither should your logic be allowed to dominate. Overreliance on logic can lead to closed-mindedness and rigidity; we can become stuck in the grooves of our established thoughts and patterns, failing to see new possibilities and angles. Be willing to question your beliefs and conclusions, allowing room for intuition to bring in fresh insights.

Experiment with blending intuition and logic in decision-making scenarios. Practice weighing the relative inputs from both and making decisions based on a balanced perspective. Observe the results. Did the outcome validate your intuitive hunch, or did your logical analysis prove more accurate? Learn from these experiences and adjust your approach as needed.

Balancing intuition and logic is not something you master overnight. It's a journey of trial and error. Celebrate your success when your decisions are spot-on. When they aren't, remember that every situation offers a chance to grow, learn, and refine your approach.

This balance between intuition and logic feeds into what we mentioned earlier about the heart and mind connection. As you further progress on this path, you'll start to realize that the heart's intuitive wisdom and the mind's logical structuring can indeed work as a unified powerhouse. It all adds up beautifully, and the journey becomes all the more exciting once you realize that you're not juggling or comparing opposites, but harmonizing essential components of a balanced thought process.

The beauty of this balance lies in its potential to enhance your personal power. You learn to welcome and interpret the signals of your intuition and mix that insight with sound logic. This balanced way lends itself to more nest decision-making, creative problem-solving, and a holistic understanding of yourself and the world around you pertinent to achieving your desires.

As you learn to unconsciously integrate intuition and logic, you'll notice life becoming inherently fuller and richer. You'll start making choices that are better adjusted to your deepest desires and truest reality. Your journey towards abundance will be smoother and more satisfying because you're not only using your cerebral intelligence but also engaging in the deeper, instinctive wisdom innate within you. It's a powerful, beautiful synergy that's yours to explore and harness.

In the next step, we shall dwell further into creating an inner unity that embodies a balanced intuition and logic, further harmonizing heart and mind. With a strong mind under your control feeding off a balanced intuition and logic, you'll be less reactive to circumstances and instead become a proactive creator of your own life. It's a fascinating study and it only gets better from here.

Chapter 3

The Symphony of Inner Unity

Having explored the realms of both our hearts and minds, we're now poised to harmonize these two potent forces into what can be envisioned as a symphony of unity—where each instrument, no matter how different, contributes to a melodious whole. This harmony we're talking about transcends mere balance. It is about reveling in the yin and yang of our inner unity, where the profound wisdom of our hearts and the untapped power of our minds intermingle to create a life of alignment, fulfillment, and abundance. This oneness enables the quiet music of our hearts to rise above the often overwhelming noise of our thoughts. It's a case where the sum is indeed greater than its parts; when our heart and mind unite, they magnify the potential of what we can be, do and achieve. This inner unity can serve as a compass guiding us toward the life we truly desire, a life rich in health, love, prosperity, and joy. Once we master this symphony of unity within ourselves, every beat of our heart and every thought in our minds becomes a conscious choice in the direction of our abundant, authentic life.

Harmonizing Heart and Mind

The journey towards inner unity is about bringing together two of humanity's greatest resources - the heart and the mind. While these two powerhouses often operate differently, achieving a harmony between the mind's analytical prowess and the heart's innate wisdom can catalyze transformation and abundance in unforeseen ways.

Distancing from the noise of everyday life and centering ourselves allows us to appreciate the symphony that both the heart and the mind can craft together. Imagine your heart as a musical instrument, the ink that pens the lyrics of your true emotions. On the other hand, see your mind as the composer that intricately designs the harmonies to align this emotional symphony.

The first step towards harmonizing the heart and mind is to acknowledge their individual value. The heart, typically associated with emotion and compassion, holds data vital to our decision-making process. Its intuitive and empathetic characteristics urge us to react based on our core values and ideals rather than immediate circumstances. Meanwhile, the mind, associated with logical and rational thought, helps us analyze, plan, and organize. It filters the heart's emotional data giving us the capacity to implement and actualize our potential. Respect for the unique capabilities of both these entities is the origin point of their harmonization.

Acknowledging your heart and mind separately allows a greater understanding of the dialogue between them. Often, we feel conflicted because this dialogue becomes a heated debate, with the heart advising one direction and the mind pointing to another. This internal tug-of-war can drain your energy and cloud your judgment.

Harmony comes from acknowledging the tug-of-war and deciding to let the string slacken. It's OK to let emotions flow without immediately seeking rational explanation from the mind. Similarly, it's fine to allow the mind to wander, brainstorm, and analyze without initially anchoring it to emotion. Give both the heart and the mind their respective space and allow them to function independently before seeking alignment.

Once you value the heart and mind's individual contributions, the next step is to encourage collaboration. Encourage the heart to share its emotional narrative while the mind listens and absorb these feelings empathetically. Then, let the mind construct a logical pathway as the heart listens and embraces this process. This is a conscious effort to keep the conversation between the heart and mind balanced, fair, and open.

An effective method of encouraging this collaboration is through meditation. Meditation brings calm to the internal dialogue by silencing the noise and focusing on the rhythm of your heartbeat or your breath. When you're present and aware, you tune into the heart's wisdom while simultaneously employing the mind's keen observation and receptive listening. You'll find answers flowing through you, which naturally integrate emotion and logic. You might surprise yourself at how the heart and mind arrive at the same conclusions when they're allowed to converse calmly.

Another technique is journaling, providing a tangible trail of your thoughts and emotions. Journaling is a solace where your heart can pour its feelings, and your mind can follow with a comprehensive analysis. This therapeutic method enables you to visually witness the harmonious dance between your heart and mind.

Then there's the practice of mindfulness, a tool that can promote active cooperation between the mind and heart. By focusing on the present moment, you grant space for emotional and logical comprehension to process concurrently. This acceptance of 'what is' allows you to navigate life genuinely, without the constant battle between heart-urged decisions and rationally-devised plans.

Cultivating kindness towards oneself is a defining factor in achieving this balance. Remember, harmonizing the heart and mind isn't about forming a perfect union where they agree all the time—it's about creating a space where both entities respect, listen to, and learn from each other. If you perceive discrepancies as an opportunity for growth rather than a problem to be solved, the path towards harmony becomes less strenuous and more enlightening.

In this journey of harmonization, you may experience resistance, surprises, and profound insights. Remember, both your mind and heart have been conditioned by life experiences and their protective instinct may cause initial resistance to change. But with patience and repeated conscious communication, they can learn to harmonize, trust, and complement each other effectively.

One cannot simply ask the heart to stop feeling or the mind to stop thinking. It's about balancing their input. When the heart and mind learn to sing the same song, it strengthens the symphony of inner unity, leading you to your true abundance potential.

Once you fine-tune your heart and mind to play in harmony, the results can be beautiful and life-altering. It can open the doors to a true sense of peace, confidence, and abundance. As you navigate through life, your harmonized heart and mind become a light guiding you towards choices that align with your desired abundance in health, relationships, finance or any other forms of prosperity.

These balanced decisions from a harmonized heart and mind act as catalysts for the life you desire. Once your heart and mind start sharing the same rhythm, they produce a melody so potent it can attract abundance into your life like a magnet. As you venture towards the path of integrated living, you'll experience the symphony of inner unity, setting the stage for a more fulfilling, abundant life.

The Yin and Yang of Inner Unity

As we delve into the depths of our inner harmony, we can't ignore the concept of Yin and Yang. The ancient Chinese philosophy that speaks of the balance of opposing, yet complementary, forces. The Yin is passive, dark, feminine, and receptive, while the Yang is active, light, masculine, and projective. This dynamic balance is all around us — day and night, hot and cold, high and low. And more importantly, it exists within us, too, resonating in the dance between our hearts and minds.

Just like Yin and Yang, our heart is receptive and our mind can be projective. One feels, the other reasons. One operates from intuition, the other from logic. This dichotomy is not meant to create an internal battle, but rather work in harmony to lead us towards our greater selves. The challenge and the art lie in balancing the Yin and Yang, harnessing their individual strengths to create a unified whole — inner unity, the essence of our journey.

In order to truly understand and appreciate the splendor of this balance, one must first engage with each side separately. Have you ever sat in silence, just feeling the emotions that arise from deep within your heart, letting them flow freely, acknowledging and honoring them? This is connecting with your Yin, your intuitive side that gives voice to your feelings, providing an authentic sense of who you are.

But, organizing those feelings into thoughts and actionable items is the part your Yang, your rational mind, plays. It illuminates your path by providing structure to your Yin's raw emotional state. Ideas, questions, and plans formulate themselves as your Yang swings into action. Your Yang projects and pushes forward those things your Yin has highlighted as essential to your being.

This interplay rings the symphony of inner unity. Neither force is complete without the other. Without the Yin, there would be no feelings to guide us, no intuition to lead. Without the Yang, we wouldn't have the necessary structure to put our realizations into practice. Harnessing the power that comes from blending these two subsystems brings wholeness, leading to personal growth and abundance, in every sense imaginable.

It's essential to remember, that like Yin and Yang, our heart and mind are not competing forces either. They are complementary halves of the whole, striving to work together - full of potential and promise.

The power they hold together can only be unleashed by aligning them, by letting their rhythms resonate together.

So how do we successfully achieve this inner unity, this balance between our Yin and Yang? It starts with awareness. This awareness involves an understanding of the emotions from the heart and the structured thoughts from the mind. More importantly, it consists of the will to align these two elements. It's not just about coordination, it's about synergy.

Encourage dialogue, embrace the disparate entities within yourself. Feel the pulse of your Yin as it takes from the world, reacts, and changes. This intuitive side of yourself will provide an abundance of emotional data, which then the Yang is invited to assess and act upon. Allow your heart to feed its findings to your mind for clear-cut action plans.

There will be times when your Yin and Yang seem at odds, when your heart pulls you one way and your mind pushes you another. Let this not distress you. Remember, this is a dance – a dance of Yin and Yang, heart and mind. Sometimes one will take the lead, and sometimes the other. But they are dancing together, striving for harmony and balance. And it is this dance that issues forth the melody of the inner unity.

To dance, one must listen to the music. Be present, be mindful. Pay attention to your heart and mind. Acknowledge the different voices that contribute to your symphony. Relish the interplay, the transitions, and the solos. Let them inspire you to create your own unique dance of inner unity.

Embrace the Yin and Yang of inner unity. Make space for emotional agility, let yourself feel, and also think. Decipher the codes your Yang mind has interpreted to ensure the authenticity of your Yin heart. Do not attempt to suppress one for the other. For it is through their togetherness that the symphony of the inner self reaches a crescendo, sparking the flame of wholeness and abundance within you.

Last but not least, remember to be kind to yourself during this process. It's a journey, not a race. Try to be patient and gentle as you navigate the dance between your inner Yin and Yang towards a melody of harmony.

Remember, each step, each note has a purpose that will guide you towards your abundant life.

Chapter 4

Enriching Your Life with Prosperity

As we continue this journey, let's gently shift our attention to prosperity. Prosperity is more than mere material wealth; it's an enriching state of abundance that sings across all areas of your life – finance, relationships, health, and beyond. Though it's often overlooked, a crucial step towards this prosperous life is aligning your heart and mind. Too often, your mind might conceive what the heart isn't prepared for; or the heart might yearn for what the mind finds irrational. However, in this beautiful symphony of inner unity, which we set the stage for in the previous chapters, your heart and mind can collaborate. They can create a powerful energy, fuelled by your deepest emotions, ambitions, and convictions, that propels you steadily towards prosperity. Manifesting abundance requires more than just thinking or wishing; it requires feeling, believing, and immersing yourself in the energy of abundance wholeheartedly. When your heart's desire and your mind's vision harmonize, the Universe responds with synchronicity, opening the doors to a wealth of opportunities for you to flourish and thrive. So, as we delve into this chapter, we encourage a tireless dedication to practicing this alignment and nurturing the powerful energy of your emotions. Remember, prosperity is not an external treasure to chase after but an internal state of being to cultivate. By aligning the heart and mind, we can tap into this fertile soil within us, sowing the seeds of prosperity, and nurturing them with intention, until they come to full, rich, beautiful bloom.

Aligning Heart and Mind for Prosperity

The alignment of our heart and mind is a critical step towards attaining prosperity in any form, be it wealth, relationships, or health. Whether you are seeking financial success or longing for more profound, enriching human connections, alignment is key. Let's delve into this dynamic interplay and see how we can better harmonize our thoughts and emotions to foster abundance.

The first thing to understand is that the heart and mind are not two separate entities but parts of a beautiful whole, interconnected and dependent on each other. You might perceive the heart as the seat of your emotions and your mind as the center of intellectual activities. The heart symbolizes compassion, empathy, and intuition, while the mind represents thoughts, ideas, and reasoning. Neither is superior. Both are essential for personal growth and prosperity.

Consider prosperity as a river. When the heart and mind, like two strong banks, are well-aligned, the river of prosperity flows smoothly. A mind that entertains creative solutions and a heart that fuels passion make an unbeatable combination. Any form of abundance sought is readily manifested when these extraordinary forces are well-aligned.

Aligning the heart and mind begins with awareness. It involves acknowledging the emotions radiating from your heart and the thoughts sprouting from your mind. Such awareness brings clarity as you start recognizing your desires, goals, and ambitions, all essential in the path of prosperity.

Importantly, the alignment does not mean suppressing either heart's sentiments or mind's thoughts. It's about recognizing the heart's dreams and coupling them with the mind's pragmatism. It's a give-and-take relationship, where emotions enrich thoughts, and thoughts provide structure to emotions. This harmonious relationship can guide you towards attaining prosperity.

Now, you might question - How exactly can we achieve this alignment? It starts with candid heart-to-heart conversations, accepting who you are, and understanding what truly motivates you. Answer some soul-searching questions. What stirs your heart? What inspires your mind? What's your deepest longing? These cogitations can help you sort out what prosperity means to you, first and foremost.

Search for balance. Encourage thoughts that echo your heart's content. Likewise, foster feelings that resonate with your intellectual understanding. When your thoughts and feelings align, they create a powerful energy that attracts prosperity. It's a balanced state where mind and heart work in harmony, without conflict or division.

Meditation is an extremely useful practice to foster heart-mind alignment. It is a quiet, mindful activity that helps to unravel your subconscious drives, anxieties, and desires. As you delve deeper into the practice, you'll notice how much quieter the noise between our thoughts and emotions can become and how much easier it becomes to align your heart and mind.

Visualization techniques too can make a profound impact. They act as a bridge between the heart's desires and mind's logic. The heart dreams, and the mind envisages it, thus creating a blueprint for prosperity. Imagine your life as you want it to be - abundant and fulfilling. Capture the feelings, sensations, and thoughts associated with it, and keep them at the forefront of your heart and mind.

Finally, cultivate an attitude of self-love and acceptance. The heart and mind often become misaligned due to internal conflicts, guilt, or shame. However, when you love and accept yourself unconditionally, these conflicts start to fade away. You'll start feeling a sense of inner unity and alignment, a necessary factor in attracting prosperity.

Remember that the alignment journey will be unique for each one of us, and that's perfectly okay. It's a personal path you embark upon, gradually merging your thoughts and emotions with love, patience, and understanding. Remember to celebrate little victories along the way and trust the process wholeheartedly.

To sum up, aligning your heart and mind isn't a one-time task. It's a continuous process that requires daily practice, patience, and self-awareness. It's about reaching a state where your heart's desires and mind's plans are universally aligned, creating a powerful energy that magnetically attracts prosperity. It's a beautiful symphony of inner unity where each note enriches and uplifts the other. As you align, you glide; into a world abundant with possibilities and prosperity.

The Powerful Energy of Emotions

Emotions hold powerful energy that can fuel our drive towards prosperity and abundance. Recognizing, understanding, and harnessing this energy forms the crux of dealing successfully with our heart and mind alignment. It's about learning the language of emotions and deciphering its messages.

One might ask, "How exactly do emotions influence our path to prosperity?" Here's a simple explanation: Emotions steer our thoughts and actions. Every emotion we feel creates a ripple effect that influences our decisions and behaviors. When we understand the incredible energy contained within each emotion, we can start to channel it positively to drive prosperity.

It's important, however, not to mistake this for suppression or denial of negative emotions. All emotions, be it joy or sorrow, have a place in our lives. They give color to our experiences and contribute to our unique journey. Emotions aren't good or bad; they're merely indicators, pointing us to areas of our lives that require attention.

Take fear, for example. Often seen as a negative emotion, fear can be an empowering tool once we learn how to harness its energy. Fear signals potential risk, but it also encourages caution and instigates the development of contingency plans. In this way, it serves as a survival instinct that protects and prepares us.

Then there's the energizing emotion of joy, which exudes positivity, invigorates us, and propels us to move towards our dreams and aspirations. Joy, love, and gratitude create a strong, positive energy force that magnetizes abundance and prosperity.

So how do we harness the powerful energies of our emotions? The first step is awareness. By tuning in and acknowledging our feelings, we open a dialogue with our heart and mind. This emotional awareness creates a bridge between our inner and outer worlds, allowing us to truly comprehend our needs, desires, and personal values.

Sometimes, our emotions might lead us down unexpected paths, opportunities, and experiences that ultimately enrich our lives. Emotions are mysterious, yet honest mirror reflections of our inner world. They constantly inform us about our steady alignment or disalignment with our life's desires.

In order to tap into the prosperous energy it offers, we need to be honest with ourselves about what we're really feeling. Feeling your feelings is not about judging yourself, it's about understanding and acknowledging your emotional state.

Next, practicing mindfulness and presence helps us to stay attuned to our emotions as they rise and fall. Much like observing the ebb and flow of tides, we can learn to ride out the waves of our emotions. When we resist them, they persist, often manifesting in unproductive or destructive ways. Yet, when we learn to flow with them, they pass naturally, giving us insight, resolution, and renewed energy.

Finally, remember that transformation doesn't happen overnight. It requires time, consistency, and patience. Your emotions are a treasure trove of energy, waiting to be tapped and transformed. With mindfulness, acceptance, and understanding, we can learn to wield them as a powerful force for change and prosperity.

As you continue on this journey, you'll notice a burgeoning confidence in your ability to navigate your emotions, to tune into their energies, and to channel this energy towards all the abundance that you desire. You'll find yourself in harmony with your heart and mind, pulling you magnetically towards a life that's truly prosperous.

Remember, emotions are part of our human experience, and we can learn to harness their energy to create abundance in our lives. It's our choice whether to view this emotional energy as a hindrance or as a benefactor paving our road to prosperity. So let's take the plunge, dive deep, and learn to swim in the powerful energy of emotions to create a life of prosperity we envision.

Chapter 5

The Art of Emotions Monitoring

As we venture further into our quest for harmony and abundance, our exploration takes us to a critical element shaping the tone and tenor of our lives: our emotions. Emotions illuminate our heart's desires, reflect the state of our mind, and both subtly and powerfully shape our experiences. So, the ability to mindfully observe, understand, and guide these emotions – this art of emotions monitoring – is profoundly significant. This passive and active examination of emotions allows you to recognize and acknowledge your feelings without becoming overwhelmed by them. You'll begin to see the distinct role emotions play, whether they're serving you as alerts, indicators, or barometers of your inner world. With this understanding, you're better able to cultivate emotions that align with your vision of abundance. Soon, you'll find the joy in amplifying positive emotional frequencies like love, gratitude, joy, and excitement, making these more than fleeting moments, but rather a chronic state of being. The art of emotions monitoring, therefore, isn't about simply noting that we 'feel', but creating a heartspace where positivity thrives, nudging you that much closer to your desired abundance.

The Importance of Monitoring How You Feel

Emotion monitoring isn't about throttling down the emotions we deem negative, or spurring the ones we consider positive into hyperdrive. Rather, it's about being aware of all emotions—joy and sadness, anger and love, fear and courage—and understanding their implications in your life. As with our physical wellbeing, our emotional health requires attention to maintain balance and foster growth. Negligence in this aspect can create inner chaos and bring discord in life areas we yearn abundance.

So why is it imperative to monitor your emotions? Why not just let them come and go as they please? The reason lies in the potent influence emotions wield over your mind and your actions. Our feelings are powerful drivers of behavior. They influence how we think, react and interact with the world around us. Understanding and managing these feelings can be the difference between living reactively versus living proactively.

Taking the time to identify and process your feelings empowers you to take charge of your mental and emotional states. It can help you to navigate challenges more constructively, reduce stress and anxiety, and enhance your relationships. This is where the art of emotional monitoring comes into play.

Regularly tuning into how you feel equips you with relevant information about yourself and the world around you. It is like being an emotional meteorologist, understanding the weather patterns of your inner universe. This awareness eases the identification of emotional patterns, triggers, and habits that may be encouraging or deterring your aim to create abundance in various life areas.

Some feelings are reliable indicators that a situation or a person may not be conducive to us while others reveal that we are on track towards positive growth. For example, recurrent feelings of unease or tension show that there is an aspect in life we need to address or a situation requiring change for better alignment with our desires.

Whereas, feelings of peace or happiness indicate alignment with our true self and aspirations.

Poorly understood or unattended feelings can lead to emotional imbalance, causing setbacks in relationships, health, finances, or overall wellbeing. Emotional imbalance is like clutter in your home—it blocks the smooth flow of energy and can create undesirable experiences. Regular monitoring and management of feelings are akin to home cleaning, ensuring only beneficial energy circulates within and attracts positive outcomes.

Another crucial aspect of emotional monitoring involves understanding the connection between your thoughts and feelings. One precedes and influences the other. Being aware of this link empowers you to cultivate life-enhancing thoughts and, consequently, emotions that support your journey towards abundance.

Moreover, an awareness of your emotions can boost your empathy, understanding, and patience—towards others and yourself. Deepening these qualities cultivates healthier relationships, broadens your perspective, and fosters a nurturing environment for personal growth. Remember, achieving abundance often requires harmonious relationships and holistic personal development, both of which rely heavily on emotional understanding.

Recognizing the significance of your emotional fluctuations isn't just about achieving personal goals or transformation; it also concerns fostering emotional wellness. Emotional unemployment or stagnancy can be as detrimental to your wellbeing as physical lethargy. Maintaining your emotional health is equally crucial as ensuring your physical wellbeing, promoting overall harmony and balance in life.

It can be a challenge to stay attuned to the undercurrent of emotions amidst the hustle of daily life. However, this shortage of time can't be an excuse for ignorance. Indeed, it's more reason to make emotional monitoring a vital part of your routine. A consistent practice paves the way for identifying any emotional imbalances swiftly and addressing them before they escalate.

Furthermore, remember that all emotions have a place in our life's tapestry—they are not inherently good or bad. They serve as messengers of your internal world, signaling what needs attention and what's working well. Don't shy away from any emotional state; honor it for its existence and the lesson it brings. Your moments of sadness and joy, anger and love, fear and courage all contribute equally to shaping your unique journey towards an abundant life.

In conclusion, the practice of monitoring your emotions offers deep insights into your inner self, strengthens emotional health, and crucially, facilitates the alignment of thoughts and feelings with your desired abundance. Keep in mind, your emotions don't control your destiny; you do. By understanding and managing your emotions, you become the master of your own life, sculpting it into the abundant masterpiece that you envision.

In the following section, measures for cultivating positive emotional frequencies will be further explored, offering you practical strategies to nurture emotions that support your journey towards abundance. Though the terrain of emotions can be challenging to navigate, remember that each step you take in understanding your emotions is a leap towards your abundant life.

Cultivating Positive Emotional Frequencies

Your emotional frequencies play a large role in shaping your reality. They can influence your energy levels, mental clarity, and even your interactions with others. That's why it's essential to cultivate positive emotional frequencies.

Cultivating positive emotional frequencies starts with understanding your emotions. Realize that emotions are complex and multi-dimensional. They aren't just positive or negative in nature but a spectrum of experiences that shape and reinforce your worldview.

The first step in cultivating positive emotional frequencies is to acknowledge that all emotions are valid. Even so-called 'negative' emotions have their place. They can serve as a catalyst for transformation, prompting us to investigate aspects of our lives that may need change. Suppressing or denying any emotion can lead to internal imbalance and discord.

Essentially, it's about managing and responding to your emotions rather than trying to control them. Be open to your feelings, treat them with respect, and they can become powerful allies in your journey towards a more abundant life.

The second step is to learn to navigate your emotional landscape consciously. You can do this by regularly checking in with yourself and identifying your emotional state. In doing so, you cultivate greater self-awareness and mind-heart coherence, attuning yourself to the frequencies that best serve your well-being.

A key aspect of this process is mindfulness - the practice of being fully present and engaged in the present moment without judgment. With mindfulness, you can observe your feelings without getting caught up in them, allowing you to maintain a balanced emotional state despite external influences.

To hone your mindfulness skills, consider practicing meditation. Meditating regularly can be instrumental in cultivating positive emotional frequencies. It can help you establish a deeper connection with your inner self, making it easier to recognize and release negative emotional patterns.

Another practice for cultivating positive emotional frequencies is gratitude. Focusing on the positives in your life can redirect your emotional energy and help you stay attuned to abundance. Incorporating a daily gratitude practice, such as keeping a gratitude journal, can significantly improve your outlook on life.

Gently replacing negative thought patterns with positive affirmations can also influence your emotional frequency. Regularly repeating affirmations can condition the mind to align with positive emotions, effectively transforming your inner dialogue and emotional landscape over time.

Consistently nurturing your well-being through practices such as exercise, proper nutrition, and quality sleep are also fundamental. By taking care of your physical health, you are in a better position to sustain positive emotional states, leading to a balanced and harmonious frequency.

Surrounding yourself with positive influences is another powerful way to cultivate positive emotional frequencies. Positive people, environments, literature, and other uplifting elements can contribute to your frequency. Remember, like attracts like in the world of frequencies.

Cultivating positive emotional frequencies is not a one-time occurrence. It is an ongoing, dynamic process of growth and transformation. It takes time and practice, so be patient with yourself. Take one step at a time, celebrate your victories, and remember to enjoy the journey as much as the destination.

In conclusion, cultivating positive emotional frequencies is instrumental in aligning your heart and mind for prosperity. It's not about always being happy, but rather being in tune with your feelings, acknowledging and learning from them, and shaping them into resources for personal growth.

Ultimately, aligning your emotional frequencies positively enhances your ability to tap into the abundance in all areas of your life. So, start cultivating those positive emotional frequencies, and step into the life of abundance that awaits you.

Chapter 6

The Practice of Mindfulness

Right after the beneficial and healing work we've been through with monitoring our emotions, we now move towards the practice of mindfulness. If emotions are the colors of our life, mindfulness allows us to become the artist, fully present and intentional with every brushstroke. The importance of being in the present moment cannot be overstated. Mindfulness, far from being ancillary, is a cornerstone of our journey towards abundant life. Not only does it hone our awareness of our emotional frequencies, but it also aids in quieting the cacophony of conflicting thoughts that can rob us of our peace. By employing mindfulness techniques, we can gradually train ourselves to stay centered in the now, to let go of past regrets and future anxieties. It's a gentle but persistent reminder that life happens in the present—that's where the magic is. What you'll find with consistent practice is that the quality of your life improves significantly; even mundane tasks sparkle with a newfound vivacity. And when we become mindful, our everyday tasks become more meaningful, amplifying the abundance of joy in our lives. But remember; like all precious skills, mindfulness requires dedication, patience, and practice. And as we move forward, we will delve into a variety of mindfulness exercises and ways to seamlessly integrate them into your daily routine. So, let's delve in and find beauty in every moment, making the world our canvas to create the abundant life we seek.

The Importance of Being Present

The concept of Being Present, in essence, means giving complete focus and awareness to the current moment, fully embracing the here and now. This may seem straightforward, but in truth, it is often more challenging than it appears. We live in an era of multitasking and endless distractions, where our thoughts are routinely scattered among past regrets and future anxieties. Living in this continuous state detracts from the richness and beauty that the present moment holds.

Being present is not just about focusing on the task at hand or letting go of past and future worries. It means deeply immersing ourselves in each fleeting moment, accepting it fully, without judgment or resistance. Often, we're so busy thinking about the next step, we forget to appreciate the current one.

The importance of being present lies in its capacity to transform our lives. Being present primes us for more profound connections with ourselves and the world around us. When we are genuinely present, we become more in tune with our own feelings, leading to greater self-understanding. It lets us live our lives more intentionally, thereby opening the doors to a deeper sense of fulfillment.

When you're not present, you're essentially sleepwalking through life, missing out on the richness and depth of experience that each moment presents. There's a cost to this. The cost is a life that is at best, superficial, and at worst, unfulfilled and unexamined. It unfolds without us genuinely being a part of it, passing by like a blur, and gone before we even notice.

Being present allows us to experience life in high definition. It's like upgrading from a small black-and-white TV to a large-screen, technicolor one. Suddenly, there's so much more to see and feel. Life becomes a richer, fuller experience. We begin to notice details that we might have overlooked before: the smell of fresh coffee in the morning, the rustle of leaves underfoot, the smile of a stranger walking by.

Not only does being present enhance our experiences, it also improves our relationships. When we are present with others, be it during a conversation or just sitting quietly in the same room, we are attuning ourselves to them. We're listening fully, engaging completely, and showing them that they matter. This builds trust, intimacy, and fosters the type of deep connections that people are inherently wired to seek.

Additionally, being present is crucial for our mental and emotional well-being. It reduces mental clutter and cultivates inner peace. It can help mitigate stress and anxiety by pulling us away from the worries of the past and the fears of the future and bringing us back into the calmness and serenity of the present moment. It encourages us to respond to life's challenges with a clear mind and open heart instead of reacting impulsively out of fear or old patterns.

Moreover, being present opens the door to mindfulness. Mindfulness is the practice of being deeply in tune with our thoughts, feelings, and bodily sensations in each passing moment. It is about experiencing life as it unfolds, without mental commentary or harsh judgement. In essence, mindfulness is being wholly engaged with the full spectrum of life – the good, the bad, the mundane, and the awe-inspiring. It is what allows us to truly live in the present moment.

Therefore, bridging the gap between understanding the concept of being present and implementing it into your life is not an easy task and can be overwhelming. Yet, it is a worthy endeavor for the significant benefit it holds in embracing the full essence of life. It's an ongoing journey, not a destination. You don't automatically become permanently present. It's a practice you cultivate every day, with every breath, with every step.

As you embark on this journey of presence, remember that it's not about eradicating thoughts, but about developing a healthier relationship with them. It's not about always being calm and peaceful, but about courageously facing life whatever state it may be in. And finally, it's not about escaping reality, but about fully immersing yourself in it.

Appreciating the importance of being present fundamentally shifts the way we approach life. It invites us to fully live, love, and engage, thereby, allowing us to truly align with the abundant life we desire. Whether it's financial prosperity, enriching relationships, improved health, or other forms of abundance, being present is the key that unlocks the gate to the life we yearn for.

Last but not least, the practice of being present constitutes a foundational element in developing a harmonious union between your mind, heart, and spirit. The act of presence amplifies your alignment, propelling you closer to the life of abundance you desire. In effect, being present allows abundance to flow, setting the stage for the expansiveness we're all capable of possessing. It allows an unfolding of ourselves in the most authentic way possible, ultimately leading to personal growth and transformation.

So, let go of the past, stop worrying about the future, and embrace the present moment. It's a gift waiting to be unwrapped and cherished. It's where reality happens. It's where life unfolds in its full intensity and mystery. It's where true abundance lies. Breathe, embrace the present, and let abundance enrich your life.

Mindfulness Techniques and Exercises

Let's dive into an array of approaches you can consciously take to invite mindfulness into your everyday life. Each of these exercises and techniques can take you a step forward into that coveted state of being, where your emotions, thoughts, and desires are synchronized, leading you toward the abundance you yearn for.

The first in our chest of tools is quite literal: **Body-scan meditation**. A time-tested form of mindfulness exercise that can be a game-changer. It comprises becoming hyper-aware of your physical being, in an organized manner, starting maybe from your toes, traveling up your legs, meandering through your torso, and finally reaching your facial features. As you mentally survey each segment, concentrate on every sensation you feel, but refrain from judging or analyzing. The objective is simple: to be thoroughly present.

Next up, we invite you to practice the **Five Senses Exercise**. The purpose of this is to anchor you in your immediate environment, offering you a retreat from the labyrinth of your thoughts. Simply identify one thing you can taste, two you can smell, three you can touch, four you can see, and five you can hear. This exercise acts as a grounding wire, leaving you refreshed and vigilant.

Don't let the simplicity of **mindful eating** fool you; it brings about a world of transformation. Every bite is an opportunity to take notice of the textures, smells, and tastes of your food. By savoring each bite, you bring yourself entirely into the moment, thereby training your brain to be present. This practice extends beyond your meal to other facets of life—you'll find that you'll start to pay attention to the present moment in all your activities.

Another thought-provoking mindfulness exercise is **noting meditation**. As thoughts arise during your meditation, casually acknowledge them by attaching a virtual label. If it's a feeling, note it as a feeling; if it's a thought, note it as thinking. Please don't delve into details or over-complicate it. The objective is to maintain an objective outlook towards your thoughts and emotions.

A profound technique is **mindful journaling**. This involves documenting your thoughts and emotions candidly. It can be an open dialogue with yourself, a space where you can express without the fear of judgment or misunderstanding. Not only does it help record your journey, but it also quietly nudges you towards mindfulness.

When you engage in **loving-kindness meditation**, you consciously send goodwill and positivity out into the universe. Start by directing these wishes towards yourself, gradually extending it to a loved one, a neutral acquaintance, someone you have disagreements with, and finally, all sentient beings. This practice allows you to cultivate compassion and connect with others on a deeper level, bringing you one step closer to unity.

Another sensory experience you can try is a **mindful walk.** As you undertake a stroll, tune into your environment. Feel the wind on your face and the ground under your feet. Notice each step you take and how it connects with the earth. In each footfall and each breath of fresh air, there's mindfulness to be found.

Guided meditation is another potent and accessible technique that often provides a good starting point for beginners. There are countless apps and audio resources available that will calmly guide your thought process, leading you to a state of mindfulness. You just need to trust, relax, and follow the lead.

A gripping method to cultivate mindfulness is through **Yoga.** The sheer focusing power of Yoga can transform not only your physical fitness but also your mental resilience. It unifies your mind-body interaction, opening up a freeway to mindfulness.

Finally, you can also practice **mudras**, which are hand gestures used in meditation. Each gesture is tied to different qualities such as fearlessness, wisdom, or enlightenment. The act of positioning your hands and focusing on the qualities they represent can help maintain a steady, mindful attention.

It's important to remember that these exercises are not magical potions but tools. Often, the transformation is subtle, a gradual shift towards a more conscious being. Patience and persistence are indispensable companions on this journey.

Moreover, there's no one-size-fits-all in mindfulness practices. Everyone's journey is unique, so feel free to experiment with these exercises and maintain what resonates with you.

Whether you're just beginning or you're seasoned in mindfulness practice, these exercises offer a profound opportunity to deepen your understanding of yourself and your interaction with the world. Their simplicity and accessibility can seamlessly help you merge mindfulness into your daily life.

Remember, all it takes is the first step, the first breath, the first act of truly being present and aware. As you explore the different techniques and exercises, you'll uncover a much deeper connection with yourself, and you'll find the sync you've been seeking.

Integrating Mindfulness into Daily Life

After understanding the importance of being present and learning various mindfulness techniques, it's now time to delve deeper into how to integrate mindfulness into our daily lives. As we do, we'll see a remarkable shift in our experiences, our relationships, and our general outlook on life.

Mindfulness isn't a practice you limit to specific hours of your day, like a morning yoga session or a late-night journaling routine. It's an approach to living, a way of engaging with the world that transforms mundane moments into opportunities for growth and appreciation. It is a choice you make moment to moment.

Integrating mindfulness into daily life begins by setting your intention. As you wake each morning, make the conscious choice to be fully present throughout the day. This may seem challenging at first, especially in a society that encourages multitasking and constant productivity. However, like any muscle, your ability to focus and stay present will strengthen with time and practice.

Start with small, manageable chunks of time. It could be through mindful eating, paying attention to every bite, savoring the different sensations of the food, and experiencing the act of eating in a whole new way. Or you can practice mindfulness during your commute, by turning off the radio and fully diving into the experience, noticing the colors, sounds, and smells around you.

Scheduling mindfulness breaks throughout your day can also be beneficial. It could be as simple as taking five minutes to close your eyes, focus on your breathing, and clear your mind. These moments of stillness amidst the chaos of daily life ground you in the present, giving you fresh perspectives and bolstering your inner tranquility.

Remember, mindfulness isn't relegated to silence and stillness. You can also practice being present during more active parts of your day. Going for a walk? Turn it into a mindfulness exercise by observing everything around you - the shapes of the clouds, the feel of the ground beneath your feet, the sounds of the birds. A routine stroll can become an enlightening adventure.

Next, apply mindfulness to your interactions with others. How often do we speak with someone without really being present, our minds wandering off to future tasks or past events? By being fully present during conversations, we open the door for deeper connections, better understanding, and enriched relationships.

Equally vital is learning to listen mindfully. True listening involves more than hearing the words someone says. It's about paying attention to the emotions conveyed, the body language, the silences in between. Listening in such a way can change the quality of our relationships and create a compassionate space for others to express themselves.

Mindfulness can also positively impact your work life. Engaging completely in each task, rather than worrying about the future or dwelling on the past, can increase productivity and creativity. This single-minded focus can lead to better problem-solving skills and a much more satisfying work experience.

And let's not forget about integrating mindfulness into our emotional world. By becoming an aware observer of our emotions, we learn not to get swept away by them but rather see them as temporary states, arising and passing away. This perspective empowers us to respond to events in our lives with equanimity, as opposed to reacting impulsively.

Being mindful does not mean that you won't face challenges or that you'll always be in a state of peace. Rather, it provides you with the tools to handle whatever comes your way with grace and resilience.

By integrating mindfulness into every aspect of your life, from the mundane to the extraordinary, you'll find yourself more in tune with yourself and the world around you. You'll begin to experience life as a symphony of experiences, each moment precious and profound.

Finally, have patience with yourself. The journey toward a life of mindfulness is exactly that—a journey. There will be times of struggle and times of success, but each step, each breath, brings you closer to a life lived fully in the present, rich in depth and meaning.

Chapter 7

Breathing towards Inner Harmony

As we step into the realm of inner harmony, consider how the act of breathing, something we often overlook, plays a pivotal role in our path to unified heart and mind. The process of breathing, when channeled mindfully, can serve as a bridge, aligning our inner states of consciousness to facilitate alignment with the life we desire. In other words, breath has the potential to act as a tuning fork for our inner world, helping us reach the harmony we seek. This chapter introduces the concept of 'breathwork' and its role in inner alignment. Practicing and never really mastering, because it's an infinite path of self-discovery, we'll delve into specific breathwork exercises you can integrate into your daily routine. By harnessing the power of breath, you're equipping yourself with a powerful tool to redirect your thoughts, reassess your emotions, and ultimately, steer your life toward the very abundance you're seeking. Balanced inhalations and exhalations, rhythmic and focused, can become your access point to a whole new mind-heart dialogue, leading towards an inner harmony that echoes throughout every aspect of your life.

Breathwork and Inner Alignment

As we continue our journey towards inner harmony, let's delve further into the realm of breathwork. This practice is more than a process of inhaling and exhaling. It is an intricate dance of mind, body, and spirit, an avenue towards deep inner alignment.

Breathwork involves various breathing techniques designed to connect you with your inner self, cleanse your physiological and energetic systems, and help you form a bridge between your conscious and unconscious mind. Utilizing these techniques can encourage the release of unresolved emotions and limiting beliefs—those obstructions which might have been blocking you from the abundant life you desire.

Understanding the importance of inner alignment is a cornerstone for achieving abundance. Inner alignment, after all, is basically the process of orchestrating our thoughts and emotions in line with our true desires. When we align internally, we align with the flow of life. We connect seamlessly with the powerful creative energy that permeates the universe and align our vibration with that of abundance.

When we talk about our thoughts and emotions, we are essentially discussing the energy we emit into our surroundings. This energy profoundly affects our experiences and interactions. It vibrates at different frequencies and attracts experiences of similar frequencies into our lives, as per the law of attraction.

It is here that breathwork can become a powerful tool. It helps align our vibration with the frequency of abundance. By consciously changing our breathing patterns, we can effectively alter our energy frequency. This alteration can put us in a more receptive state and pave the way for attracting abundance into our life span.

Through breathwork, we can also cultivate mindfulness, a kind of nonjudgmental awareness of the present moment. It allows us to observe our thoughts and feelings as they arise, acknowledging them without reacting impulsively. This observation can help us disengage from negative thought patterns and thoughtfully choose thoughts that resonate with abundance.

Moreover, breathwork allows us to tap into worthiness and abundance. Often, we may hold onto beliefs that we are not deserving of abundance, which may manifest in feelings of guilt or inadequacy when we experience or think about the abundance we desire. Breathwork can help us release these limiting beliefs and hurdle the emotional blocks to abundance.

A few minutes of breathwork daily can also promote relaxation and reduce stress levels. Stress is a massive barrier to abundance because it puts us in a survival mode, where our focus narrows to immediate issues rather than larger goals or desires. By helping us relax and let go of stress, breathwork ushers us towards a mental space conducive to abundance.

Furthermore, breathwork also proves a potent tool in cultivating gratitude. A significant aspect of alignment is being appreciative of what we already have while inviting more. As we inhale deeply, we can learn to hold gratitude in our hearts and express it as we exhale. This cycle nurtures a relationship of appreciation with the universe, signaling our readiness for more abundance.

Through breathwork, we also find a way to heal from past wounds and traumas. Here, we acknowledge the concept of inner-child healing, which is often a critical step for many in their journey towards abundance. Traumas from our past continue to impact our present behavior and beliefs if not acknowledged and healed. Breathwork provides us a medium to sit with our inner-child, feel its emotions, and extend the healing it needs.

Through the practice of breathwork, we can discover a profound way to cleanse our energetic body. The process of conscious breathing encourages the purging of old, stuck energy that isn't serving your highest good. Releasing this stagnant energy makes space for new, abundant energy to flow in.

In conclusion, breathwork stands not just as a breathing technique but a transformative means to bolster inner alignment. It helps dissolve the barriers obstructing our path to abundance and opens doors to inner harmony. By embracing breathwork, we affirm our commitment to aligning with our higher selves, creating an internal environment where abundance can freely flow.

The practice of breathwork is a profound testament to the power we hold within ourselves- the power to shift, evolve, and step into the abundant life we deservingly seek. Are you ready to take the reins over your energy and vibrations? Stay tuned as we delve deeper into breathwork exercises in the following sections.

Breathwork Exercises

The breath is a bridge connecting the conscious and unconscious realms of the mind; it is a vital link between the physical and metaphysical worlds. Breathwork exercises, therefore, not only enhance overall wellbeing but also aid in creating inner harmony, aligning the heart, mind and spirit.

Here are some practical exercises to help guide you toward self-awareness, relaxation, and balance.

The first technique we'll explore is called 'Balanced Breathing.' Start by finding a quiet, comfortable place where you won't be disturbed. Sit or lie down in a comfortable position. This exercise involves inhaling and exhaling evenly - inhale for a count of four, hold briefly, then exhale for a count of four.

By maintaining this rhythm, you can cultivate a sense of inner balance and peace. Doing this practice regularly can help to reduce stress, clear the mind, and invite greater harmony into your daily life.

The next technique, 'Box Breathing,' is slightly more advanced but equally effective. Inhale for a count of four, hold your breath for a count of four, then exhale for a count of four, and finally, hold your breath again for a count of four. This technique creates a balanced rhythm, which can induce tranquillity, improve focus, and stabilize feelings.

Third, 'Abdominal or Belly Breathing' is an essential tool in promoting relaxation. Visualize your breath filling your belly as your abdomen expands with each inhale. On each exhale, imagine your belly contracting. This type of breathing encourages full oxygen exchange and slows down the heartbeat, which can elicit a calm, peaceful state of mind.

The '4-7-8 Breathing Technique' often referred to as the relaxing breath exercise, can help reduce anxiety and induce sleep. Inhale quietly through your nose to a count of four, hold the breath for a count of seven, then exhale through the mouth for a count of eight. This technique has a natural tranquilizing effect on the nervous system.

'Alternate Nostril Breathing,' a practice borrowed from Yoga, is known to create balance and unify the brain's dual hemispheres. Using your right thumb, close off your right nostril and inhale through your left nostril. At the peak of the inhale, close off your left nostril with your ring finger, remove your thumb from your right nostril, and exhale. Repeat this pattern, alternating nostrils after each full cycle of breath.

'Roll Breathing' is an excellent technique to promote fuller, healthier breaths, thus increasing lung capacity. The exercise involves dividing the breath into two parts. When inhaling, first fill the lower section of your lungs (as your belly expands), then shift to the upper part (as your chest rises). When exhaling, it's the same process but in reverse order.

"Coherent Breathing" is based on maintaining a breathing rate of five breaths per minute, which corresponds to the frequency of the heart's natural rhythm. Simple and profound, this technique can help bring about an immediate sense of peace and inner harmony.

Indulge in the 'Lion's Breath' to release tension in your face and chest. This somewhat unconventional technique involves taking a deep inhale through the nose, then exhaling forcefully through the mouth, stretching out your tongue towards your chin and making a 'ha' sound. It's surprisingly liberating!

Finally, remember that breathwork is not a competition or a chore. It's a process, a journey to inner harmony and balance. And like any journey, it's not about rushing to the destination but about appreciating every step along the way. Encourage yourself, be patient, and celebrate small victories.

These breathwork exercises, when integrated into your daily routine, can transform your state of mind, promote mental clarity, emotional stability, and overall wellness. By re-establishing your connection with your breath, you're empowering your instinctive self, synchronizing your thoughts, feelings, and aspiring to the abundant life you envision. Onward, to harmonious living!

Chapter 8

Embracing Your Shadows

As you continue this journey towards greater abundance, you'll realize that the path doesn't only shine with light - shadows are part of it as well. And these very shadows behoove us to understand and perform Shadow Work. This means acknowledging and integrating the aspects of ourselves that we'd rather keep hidden—the areas of shame, guilt, fear, and self-doubt. Rather than pretending they don't exist or trying to eradicate them, shadow work invites us to tenderly fold these parts back into our awareness, to welcome them home. It can seem intimidating, but the key lies in acceptance and compassion, recognizing that these shadows are not defects, but valuable, integral parts of our identity. They can bolster our personal growth when embraced, helping us develop a stronger, well-rounded self. Through dedicated shadow work exercises, you'll learn to unravel these hidden aspects, shed light on them, and ultimately harness their potential to your advantage. It's a powerful process that casts new light on everything we've discussed so far - your heart, your mind, your present moment consciousness - and provides the groundwork for true self-transformation in pursuit of an abundant life.

Understanding Shadow Work

The process of embracing our shadows often involves an understated but transformative practice known as shadow work. Central to personal growth and self-discovery, shadow work is the conscious effort to explore and integrate the darker, more hidden parts of our psyche, often referred to as our 'shadow selves'.

Our shadow selves represent the aspects we deny, repress, or ignore; the parts of us deemed "unacceptable" by societal norms or personal judgments. Shadow work is the process of bringing these hidden elements into the light, allowing us to acknowledge, accept, and essentially heal these fragmented parts of ourselves.

To understand shadow work, you need to embrace the idea that we all embody a spectrum of emotions and behaviors, ranging from joy, love, and compassion to anger, jealousy, and fear. Because of cultural, social or familial expectations, we often suppress those negative emotions or behaviors, thus they become hidden in our shadow selves.

The critical part to keep in mind about shadow work is that it is not about eliminating these negative aspects or trying to turn them into positive ones. Rather, shadow work aims to loosen the grip that repressed emotions and experiences have over our actions and reactions. Its intention is balance—understanding that we are composed of both light and dark aspects, and that accepting the whole spectrum is key to inner peace.

This form of self-discovery invites introspection and honesty. It requires courage to face our concealed fears, suppressed emotions, and denied aspects. But in doing so, shadow work can pave the way for profound personal breakthroughs by freeing us from previously unconscious, self-limiting patterns.

It's important to realize, shadow work does not mean dwelling or wallowing in our darkness. Rather, it's about bringing what's hidden into our awareness, acknowledging its presence, understanding its influence, then integrating it into our sense of self. This integration helps us become more whole, allowing us to face life more authentically and courageously.

Shadow work is, in many ways, akin to peeling back layers of an onion. It can be uncomfortable and tear-inducing, but every layer we peel back gets us closer to our authentic core. It's a process that can feel challenging and overwhelming at times, but also empowering and liberating as we begin to uncover, face, and accept these hidden aspects of ourselves.

Through shadow work, we're given the opportunity to debunk the illusions we've maintained about ourselves and to reclaim aspects of our personalities that have long been suppressed. It's about understanding that what we deem as 'negative' or 'unwanted' aspects in ourselves are simply parts of our human experience. By acknowledging, accepting, and incorporating them, we provide ourselves with a more holistic self-view.

To a sense, shadow work is like shining a light on the darkest part of the room. This darkness may be uncomfortable and perhaps scary, but once we switch on the light, the fear disappears, and we can see things as they actually are. It helps us build a deeper relationship with ourselves and increases our consciousness about ourselves and the world around us.

Remember, our shadows contain not just negative but also positive aspects of ourselves. They can capture ignored or hidden talents, suppressed desires, unfulfilled potentials, and more. So when we do shadow work, we're merely opening up a path for these rejected aspects of ourselves to shine through.

Ultimately, shadow work is about self-acceptance and self-love. It's about no longer forsaking or rejecting any aspect of ourselves, but instead embracing our shadows while integrating them into our state of consciousness. It's about balance, self-embracement, and making peace with our imperfect yet beautiful human existence.

Admittedly, shadow work is not an overnight process. It's a journey towards self-discovery and personal growth that requires courage, patience, and commitment. So, remember to give yourself grace and kindness as you embark on this path. Be gentle with yourself, understanding that every step you take makes a significant difference in your journey towards embracing your shadows.

In the next section, we'll delve into various exercises and techniques you can use to start or deepen your shadow work. Remember, it's a journey well worth undertaking, as integrating our shadows is a powerful way to bring harmony between our hearts and minds and fully align with the abundant life we desire.

Shadow Work Exercises

Shadow work, a practice steeped in acceptance and understanding, is a process that can help you integrate and heal parts of yourself that you'd usually resist or appeal to tuck away. Here are some practical exercises for you to engage in shadow work.

Firstly, **journalling** is an excellent place to begin self-exploration. Jotting down thoughts, feelings, patterns, experiences, and dreams can provide a clear understanding of yourself. Also, remember to write about situations that provoke powerful emotional responses. These could be clues to unearthing your shadow self.

Mindful meditation is another beneficial tool. During meditation, you can visualize meeting your shadow self. Dialogue with this part of yourself, ask probing questions, and cultivate a compassionate understanding of your shadow's roots. This exploration will allow for greater integration of your shadow side.

A sometimes overlooked but incredibly useful tool is **Dream Analysis**. Our subconscious mind can reveal significant insights into our shadows through our dreams. Be proactive and record your dreams, then take time to dissect them, looking for themes, emotions, and aspects that may relate to your shadow self.

Working with a **Therapist or Coach** experienced in shadow work can be a valuable experience. A professional guide can help you navigate through the emotional landscape of your shadow self and provide a safe space for your exploration.

A more unconventional, yet efficient, method is **Art Therapy**. Artistic expression can help externalize your thoughts, emotions, and your shadow side. Without the confinements of verbal language, your inner reality can find a way out more freely.

Engaging in **Inner Child Work** can be transformative in shadow work. This process involves acknowledging and healing your unresolved childhood experiences and trauma. Understanding and forgiving your past can cultivate more profound acceptance of your shadow self.

Yet another efficacious practice is **Bodywork**. Different emotions and traumas are stored within your physical body. Modalities like yoga, massage or somatic experiencing can help release these emotions and bring them to light.

The **Light Projection Exercise** can be an illuminating practice. Often, what we admire in others is what we deny in ourselves. List qualities you admire in others, understand why they are remarkable to you, then acknowledge these qualities within yourself.

Shadow Work Guided Meditations and Hypnosis are two powerful tools. They facilitate an intense dive into your inner world, guiding you through dark zones that your consciousness has hidden away.

Cultivating **Radical Honesty** with oneself is at the core of shadow work. Be honest about your flaws, mistakes, and unbecoming behaviors. Acknowledge these aspects of yourself without judgment.

The Empty Chair Technique from Gestalt therapy can also be employed. This technique allows you to project your shadow self onto an empty chair, enabling a direct dialogue with your subconscious.

Usage of **affirmations** can also prove advantageous. An affirmation like 'I willingly release the shadows and heal them, thus calling light into their place' can be quite impactful.

Introspection and Mind Mapping can aid you in recognizing triggers that prompt the appearance of your shadow self. Through this awareness, you'll be better equipped to manage your shadow self's manifestations).

Shadow work is not always pleasant, but it is an essential part of journeying toward a balanced and abundant life. Keep your heart open, be compassionate with yourself, and remember, the goal is not to eliminate the shadow self, but to understand, accept, and integrate this part of yourself within your entire being.

Chapter 9

The Power of Gratitude

After uncovering the transformative influence of shadow work, let's pivot our attention towards one of the most potent tools for inviting abundance into your life - the power of gratitude. With its simple nature, gratitude is a profound force that connects our heart and mind, creating a cycle of positivity that manifests abundance in various facets of our life. It's the heart's song of joy for what it has and a defiant resistance against the prevalent culture of lack. This heartful recognition reinforces your faith in life's benevolence. It shapes the way you perceive the world, nurturing an attitude of abundance that amplifies your receptivity to life's blessings. As an emotion, gratitude doesn't just share space with joy; they're practically twins, making you perceive and engage with your world in ways that bring more to be thankful for. By keeping a gratitude journal, you sketch the positive contours of your daily life, giving a frame to your blessings and setting the stage for more good to enter. Complementing this practice, the embodiment of gratitude through rituals strengthens its vitality within you, cementing your place in the cycle of abundance. In short, the practice of gratitude elevates your life frequencies, aligning your emotional, mental, and spiritual components to resonate with a life of abundance.

Keeping a Gratitude Journal

Cultivating gratitude can be a significant factor in aligning your heart and mind towards the life of abundance you desire. One valuable way to encourage this growth is by keeping a gratitude journal, a simple yet powerful tool in your toolkit for personal transformation.

A gratitude journal is exactly what it sounds like - a space where you can jot down what you are thankful for each day. Spending a few minutes each day documenting your gratitude can transform your mindset, helping you focus on the positive aspects of your life and bringing you closer to that desired state of abundance.

The beauty of a gratitude journal is in its simplicity. It doesn't require any special materials or a significant time commitment. All you need is a notebook and a pen, and a few minutes of contemplative peace. It's not the aesthetic of the exercise that matters, but the emotional shift it can create.

The very act of writing down what you are grateful for leads you to deliberately think about the good in your life. It brings your focus away from what might be lacking, and toward what is abundantly present. It's a powerful mental shift because what we focus on tends to increase in our perception. When we focus on abundance, it becomes more prevalent in our lives.

Naturally, there may be days when you feel as though there is little to be grateful for, especially when faced with hardship or loss. But these are the times when the practice of gratitude is most crucial. By finding even the smallest thing to be thankful for, we can begin to shift our perspective from scarcity to abundance.

The process of keeping a gratitude journal is quite straightforward. At the end of each day, designate a few minutes to reflect on what happened during the day. Allow your mind to journey back through the moments, and identify those where you felt a sense of joy, peace, or thankfulness. Write these moments down, capturing the experience and your feelings as best as you can.

It's essential to make this a regular practice, ideally daily. Consistency is key in creating any new habit, and it's through repetition that we can start to reframe our thoughts. By consistently identifying and recording our gratitudes, we essentially train our mind to notice more opportunities for gratitude throughout the day.

For those new to this practice, it might be helpful to start with simple and concrete things for which to be grateful. These can be as basic as a delicious meal enjoyed, a sunny day, or a kind gesture from a stranger. As the habit develops, you can then challenge yourself by expressing gratitude for more complex things like relationships, personal growth, or life's challenges which provide opportunities for learning and adaptation.

As you build this habit, you'll likely start to see a shift in your mindset. Your approach to life might subtly change, and you'll begin noticing more positive aspects of your environment. More importantly, over time, you may find that even during challenging times, you can spot and appreciate the small, valuable moments hidden within. And it's often during these challenging times that recognition and appreciation of these small moments bring a profound sense of peace and abundance.

While the act of keeping a gratitude journal might be simple, the effects it may have on your mental and emotional state can be profound. This simple practice will foster a mindset of abundance and help shift your thought patterns and emotional frequencies towards positivity.

Remember, gratitude is not just about being thankful for the good times but finding a reason to be thankful even during challenges. A gratitude journal should not be a vehicle for denial but rather a tool to appreciate the complete range of human experience. It's about acknowledging the good within the difficult and finding joy amidst the mundane.

Keeping a gratitude journal is an effective way to cultivate a consistent state of thankful mindfulness. As you continue to record and revisit your gratitudes, you'll find that they not only bring you a moment of joy when you experience them but continue to uplift your spirit as you recall and appreciate them. The ongoing reflection and repeated acknowledgment can lead to a sustained increase in overall gratitude, happiness, and a sense of abundance.

By infusing your daily life with gratitude, you encourage your heart and mind to tap into a deep well of abundant positivity. In this way, a gratitude journal can be an essential component in synchronizing your thoughts and emotions to align with the abundant life you desire.

Gratitude Rituals and Practices

Incorporating gratitude rituals into your life can radically reframe the way you see the world. Recognizing the bounty in our daily lives shifts our focus from what's missing to the abundance surrounding us. So, let's dive into several gratitude practices that can start invigorating your life with a heart full of appreciation.

First, the simplest practice you can begin with is saying "thank you" more. Not just for the polite gesture at a dinner party, but for everything. Thank the sun for warming your skin, the rain for nourishing the greens, the smile of a stranger, and the comfortable bed you sleep in. This might seem a little odd at first but try it out for a while, it creates a newfound respect for the smaller things around us. Always make sure to mean it, feel it.

Next, start your day with a gratitude meditation. Dedicate the initial moments of your day to consciously sit in silence, and think about 3 things you're thankful for today. Think of these things, visualize them and genuinely express gratitude towards it. It can lead to a positive start for the day, your mindset tuned into abundance and optimism.

Create a dedicated gratitude jar. This can be a playful yet powerful practice. Whenever you feel grateful for something, write it down in a small piece of paper, fold it and toss it into this jar. Over time, this jar will get filled reminding you of the piled-up blessings. On days that feel a little rough, pull out a few notes and remind yourself of all the good that still exists.

Practicing gratitude through visualization involves mentally picturing the things, people, or situations you're thankful for, and then letting that feeling of gratitude radiate throughout your body. Visualization can deeply embed the sensation of thankfulness into your subconscious mind, creating a positive shift in your overall aura and disposition.

Take some time out during the day to enjoy the gratitude walk. As you stroll, observe the beauty around you and express thanks for it. This could be nature, other human beings, architecture, or anything else that catches your eye. Walk slowly, purposefully, taking it all in. This practice not only cultivates gratitude but also helps in being more present and mindful.

Taking care of something or someone is an implicit act of gratitude. It might be a pet, a plant, or a person, by taking responsibility for their well-being, you express gratitude for their existence in your life. It nurtures your compassion, making your gratitude more profound and palpable.

Expressing gratitude towards your own body and soul is an essential practice. Too often, we forget to thank our own selves. Your body and soul do so much for you, they deserve some acknowledgment and appreciation. As you eat, thank your body for absorbing the nutrients it needs. When you exercise, thank your body for its strength and resilience. When you learn something new, thank your mind for its ability to grow and adapt.

Moreover, writing 'thank you' notes isn't a practice limited to after receiving gifts. Write thank you notes to people who made a difference in your life. It doesn't need to be something big. It could be thanking a friend for their time, or a family member for their understanding. Expressing gratitude directly like this strengthens relationships and spreads the vibrational energy of gratitude.

Then, there is sharing the gratefulness at the dinner table. Take turns in sharing what you're grateful for each day, it can be a heartwarming and bonding exercise for the family.

In addition to this, practicing 'gratitude-replacement' can be quite transformational. Whenever a negative thought creeps in, consciously replace it with something that you are grateful for. This practice helps shift the negative dominant thoughts with positive feeling of gratitude.

Another practice is 'gratitude in advance'. Here, you thank for what you desire as if it is already manifested into your life making you align with it's frequency. It's a powerful practice which makes your dreams and desires more tangible.

Furthermore, performing a bedtime ritual of jotting down the gifts of the day in your gratitude journal wraps up your day on a positive note. Reliving these moments of happiness and thankfulness can induce quality sleep as well.

Besides all these practices, it's important to understand that gratitude isn't a one-time or part-time practice, but a lifestyle. The most effective way to make gratitude a lifestyle is by finding your own flow. A practice that resonates with you in a real way, something that fills your heart with joy and thankfulness each time you do it.

To conclude, these weren't exhaustive but suggestive. The essence of a gratitude practice is in its emotion, the feeling of sincere appreciation that fills your heart. Do not just do them, feel them and gratitude will start pouring into your life from every corner.

Chapter 10

Living Abundantly

As we step into the reality of living abundantly, it's about more than simple material goods or financial coolness; it's the joy of living in harmony with your heart's desires, wrapping yourself in a blanket of peace, and soothing your soul with the lullaby of satisfaction. Here, it's about aligning your inner world so that your outer world reflects the abundance you seek. This precious alignment emerges from a glowing combination of mindful self-awareness, mindful attention, and the constant practice of gratitude, as discussed in the previous chapters. Your path to abundance is not strewn with shortcuts; it's a journey that requires discipline, patience, and a dedication to inner growth. Note the signs of a blossoming abundant life—radiating positivity, fulfilling relationships, improved mental and physical health, and a profound feeling of contentment. These signs don't just randomly appear; they're the result of deliberately sowing the seeds of abundance in your mind's fertile ground, filtering your emotions through a mesh of positivity, and allowing your actions to dance to the rhythmic pulse of your heart. You're now in the driver's seat, navigating your way towards an overflowing life, humming along to the symphony of abundance.

The Roadmap to Abundance

The journey towards abundance is not a linear path. It's more akin to a dynamic dance, an interplay between our thoughts, emotions, and the universe itself. Each step forward involves unveiling layers of growth and understanding about ourselves, culminating in the wholesome sync with our heart, mind, and the divine. Let this be your guide as you set forth on your unique and transformative journey towards abundance.

Firstly, acknowledge the power of your thoughts. Your mind is an effective creative tool, capable of manifesting your reality. Recognize your thoughts as the building blocks of your life - carefully align them with your heart's wisdom to create a life naturally abundant. But, it's not just about changing thoughts; it's about tuning in and understanding what makes you - you. Desiring a life of happiness without really understanding what happiness means to you will inevitably leave you striving for an abundance that isn't truly aligned with your deepest self.

Secondly, step into the world of emotions. Our feelings act like a beacon, guiding us towards our authentic selves, and hence, abundance. Your feelings reflect your alignment with your heart's desires and the universal rhythm. Recognizing and monitoring how you feel will direct you to live more genuinely and make decisions that lead to abundance.

Of course, to reach abundance, we need to master mindfulness. Be present in every moment, observing and accepting what unfolds without judgement. Through practices like breathwork, you can achieve inner harmony and pave the way towards abundance. Breathwork can help align the heart and mind, and clear out any emotional clutter blocking your path to prosperity.

Another key stop in our abundance journey is the shadow work. This represents the process of acknowledging and embracing all parts of yourself, including those that may be difficult to face or accept. By doing this difficult but rewarding work, you can move toward abundance with wholeness, bringing both your lights and shadows into alignment.

Moreover, developing the bridge between the heart and mind is another significant part of the roadmap. They are not separate entities but are interplay forces within you. Cultivating this unity, experiencing this inner harmony, can be transformative, affecting every aspect of our lives, and opening us up to thriving abundance.

As we journey towards abundance, we should also bear in mind that abundance is not just about having more. It's also about making the most of what we have and understanding that our potential for happiness and fulfillment doesn't exclusively rest on materials. Abundance is the richness of life in all its facets, including health, relationships, experiences, happiness, and love.

We should also realize that abundance is a continuing journey, not a final destination. As we evolve and grow, our understanding of abundance will also change. By maintaining an open heart and mind throughout the process, we welcome the freedom to cultivate and utilize abundance in whatever form it may take at each stage in our life.

Lastly, never forget to enjoy the journey. The road to abundance is as important as the destination. Each step, each realization, each moment of introspection adds richness to our lives. In this way, the journey itself is abundant. Each moment is not just a means to an end but an end itself, filled with the opportunity for joy, growth, and fulfillment.

Remember, the roadmap to abundance isn't a rigid plan; it's a gentle guide, helping you find your own way in alignment with your unique self and universe. It's an invitation to embark on the most rewarding journey you'll ever set off on - a journey to becoming who you were meant to be, experiencing life as it was meant to be experienced: abundantly.

So now, equipped with the knowledge of this roadmap, you're ready to take those steps forward. Breathe in deeply, be present in each moment, let your heart lead the way, and embrace the beautiful journey towards a life of authentic and lasting abundance.

Signs of a Harmonious and Abundant Life

Wading through the waves of life, you may not be explicitly aware that you're experiencing a harmonious and abundant life. Sometimes, it's not until we pause and reflect that we come to comprehend the tremendous prosperity that surrounds us. Here, we are going to outline some signs that indicate you're living a life in alignment with abundance.

Firstly, an unmistakable sign of abundance is having a profound sense of inner peace despite what's happening around you. Inner peace is a form of wealth that can't be purchased. It comes from an assurance that all is well, all of the time. When you recognize that life's tumults are only part of the journey and aren't here to stay, you cultivate an unshakeable sense of serenity that is a reflection of your inner harmony.

Secondly, experiencing frequent bouts of gratitude is a sign that abundance has taken root in your life. When you're living abundantly, you tend to feel a deep appreciation for everyday blessings, from the roof over your head to the food on your plate. It's an awareness that being alive is in itself an enormous gift.

Another sign is the ability to live in the moment and appreciate 'the now.' An abundant life is not fixated on past regrets or future concerns. It's soaking in the beauty of each moment, savouring the magic of the 'now' and personal growth it affords you.

Fourthly, abundance in life manifests as an overflow of joy that radiates to those around you. When you're living in abundance, you find joy not only in your accomplishments but also in the success of others. You understand that the universe has infinite resources, and someone else's gain is not your loss.

Next, an indicator of a harmonious and abundant life is having healthy, enriching relationships. The quality of these relationships doesn't depend on the number but rather on the depth and essence of these connections. These relationships champion growth, foster love, and challenge you to become better.

Material wealth, though not the primary determinant, is also a part of the abundant life equation. However, in this case, it is wealth generated not from a place of scarcity, fear, or desperation, but from patience, trust, and wisdom. It propels your dreams while contributing positively to the world.

An abundant life is additionally seen in the way you handle challenges. Difficulties and obstacles become stepping stones for progress, not stumbling blocks. You manage challenges with grace, knowing they're merely opportunities for growth.

Fostering an attitude of generosity is another sign. When you have plenty, you share plenty. It may be sharing your time, money, resources, or even sharing your knowledge. This generosity represents a heart that understands and embodies abundance.

Indeed, the hallmark of living a harmoniously abundant life is having inner contentment and fulfillment. It's believing that even with all your imperfections and mistakes, you're still enough. It's understanding that success isn't marked by accumulation but appreciation.

Moreover, embodying resilience signifies a harmonious and abundant life. It's having the refusal to let setbacks keep you down for long. You bounce back because you understand that failures are not defining, but refining moments.

Having a sense of purpose is another essential signpost. When you have a clear understanding of your purpose and passion, it adds a sense of richness to your life that is far more durable than financial wealth. It directs your actions, energies, and resources towards truly meaningful life quests.

Lastly, an abundant life is evident in the serenity that comes with authenticity. When you're free to be your true self, unapologetically and boldly, it's a sign that you're in sync with your internal values, and that's a manifestation of abundance.

Remember, signs of a harmonious and abundant life may show up differently for each of us, and that's okay. It's not the labels of what we own or achieve that determine our abundance but the manner in which our hearts and souls mediate our life experiences. So, keep tuning into the wisdom of your heart, harnessing your mind power, and practicing mindfulness. These provide the kernels that develop into a fulfilling, harmonious, and abundant life.

As you traverse your unique route toward abundance, honor your journey and know that each step is bringing you closer to realizing your harmonious and abundant life. Look out for these signs, but above all believe in the abundance that you're capable of ushering into life, for it is limitless, just as you are.

Chapter 11

Reflecting on Your Journey

In this voyage of harmonizing heart, mind, and spirit, there's much to contemplate. It's significant to pause and look back at your growth. You've discovered the wisdom of your heart, harnessed the power of your mind, and created a symphony of unity within. You've learned how to attract prosperity, monitor your emotions, and cultivate mindfulness. You've delved into your shadows, embraced gratitude, and learned to live abundantly. Recollect the transformational shifts within you, the new, empowering beliefs you've adopted, the healthy habits you've formed, and the toxic patterns you've broken. This understanding marks a significant milestone in your ongoing journey, drawing a clear path towards a future vibrant with creative energy, emotional balance, and limitless abundance. The steps you've taken so far are merely the beginning, each adding to a foundation that supports a future that is harmonious, abundant, and directly aligned with your most profound desires. Remember, the journey isn't a race or a destination, but rather a constant evolution—an endless unfolding of your highest potential and deepest authenticity.

The Ongoing Evolution of Heart, Mind, and Spirit

Your journey to living abundantly, to tapping into the wisdom of your heart and the power of your mind, and to harmonizing these elements within you, is one of continuous change—of ongoing evolution. This process is as dynamic as the universe itself, and is part of the necessary dance of growth.

In enhancing the symphony of inner unity, you've discovered that your heart and mind are not separate entities but part of a holistic system, with each component influencing and being influenced by the others. When given the opportunity, your heart and mind can work beautifully together, creating a balance between intuition and logic that propels you toward your desired existence.

The wisdom of your heart often precedes logical reasoning, and when listened to, can guide you toward choices that resonate deeply with your spirit. The heart contains an intelligence that is profound and instinctual. Harnessing this wisdom and allowing it to flow into your thought processes strengthens your internal guidance system and reinforces your trust in your decisions.

At the same time, the mind is a magnificent tool, capable of intricate analysis, creative problem-solving, and imaginative idea generation. When used effectively, your thoughts can become building blocks, facilitating the manifestation of your dreams into reality. Staying attentive to your thoughts, and consciously directing them toward what you wish to create, is a potent technique for fostering abundance in any area of your life.

The evolution of your heart, mind, and spirit requires persistent effort and a desire to live authentically. It's about finding the yin and yang of your inner unity, recognizing when to lean into intuition and when to utilize logical reasoning. The harmony created by this balanced approach promotes personal growth, understanding, and prosperity.

However, inner unity cannot exist without emotional awareness. Emotions act as powerful indicators of our spiritual health and psychological wellbeing. Monitoring your emotional frequencies and nurturing positivity encourages a positive vibration that can affect all areas of your life, from your health to your relationships, to your professional growth.

Embracing mindfulness is another crucial aspect of this ongoing evolution. Being present brings attention to the now, acknowledging current sensations and thoughts without judgment. Steadily integrating mindfulness practices into your daily routine enhances your awareness of your inner and outer worlds, providing invaluable insights into your personal journey of growth.

Aligned with this, breathwork exercises can support inner harmony and deepen mindfulness. The breath stands as a bridge between the conscious and subconscious mind, and through it, you can access tranquility and acceptance – vital ingredients for a harmonious, abundant life.

Of course, no journey is without its shadows. Accepting and understanding your shadow aspects can foster self-love and acceptance. Undertaking shadow work with courage and openness can release you from past pains and break the pattern of unconscious behavior, encouraging spiritual freedom and growth.

Gratitude too plays a significant part in our ongoing evolution. It's a powerful emotion that amplifies positive frequencies and attracts abundance. The consistent practice of gratitude nurturers an attitude of appreciation that can expand your capacity to receive and enjoy the richness of life.

The continuous evolution of your heart, mind, and spirit is a beautiful journey of discovery, acceptance, and growth. It's the shaping of your truest self, an adventure towards the realization of your innate power and wisdom and the potential for a life of profound abundance.

Therefore, with an open heart and an enlightened mind, remain committed to this ongoing evolution. It's a dynamic, experiential journey that leads to harmonious living and personal abundance. This path, intricate and glorious as it is, will guide you toward your highest potential and the true abundance that life has to offer.

A Harmonious and Abundant Future Awaits

We have journeyed together through the pathways of higher consciousness and heart-centered living, delving deep into the strategies of mindfulness, emotional monitoring, and breathwork. We've tackled the concept of shadow work with courage. We have learned to embrace gratitude as a life-affirming mantra. Now, we stand together at the exciting precipice of a harmonious and abundant future, a space filled with infinite possibilities anchored in prosperity and expansive growth. But remember, this is not an end point, but the beginning of the next phase on your spiritual and emotional journey.

This new territory may seem daunting, but it's also ripe with promise. It advances from the premise that abundance is not only about financial wealth. Instead, it beckons towards a holistic prosperity that includes fulfilling relationships, a sense of well-being, robust health, spiritual growth, and emotional stability. It's about developing a deep sense of contentment and satisfaction.

Consider the term 'harmony'. In music, it doesn't imply monotony or even the absence of discordant sounds. Instead, it speaks of diverse notes and rhythms coming together to create a beautiful melody. The same analogy applies to life. Harmony is about embracing your diverse facets, along with your triumphs and struggles. It's about fostering a balance to create a resonant tune that echoes with authenticity, self-acceptance, and love.

You have within you, the power to cultivate and live in harmony. It's not an external condition to be achieved, but an internal state to be nurtured. It needs consistent self-care, positive affirmations, and the courage to confront and manage negative emotions.

Abundance, like harmony, lies within you, waiting to be discovered. It's not about competing with others or succumbing to societal pressures of 'having more'. It's about appreciating what you have now, while being open to the flow of more prosperity. It's diving deep into the fountain of contentment that lies within you, and allowing it to permeate all aspects of your life.

Living in harmony and abundance is about adopting an integrated approach towards life. It's recognizing that your thoughts, feelings, and actions are intertwined, impacting not just your inner world, but also your external reality. It's about using this understanding to your advantage, channeling it to build a life that is fulfilling, content, and joyful.

The principles we've explored together aren't standalone concepts. They weave together, creating a symphony of positivity, deep-seated contentment, and growth. Like individual notes in a music piece, each principle complementing the other, creating an overall melody of well-being and prosperity.

Practice adopting these principles consistently. Monitor your emotions, engage in heart-centered thinking, find solace in mindfulness, and acknowledge the power of gratitude. These aren't one-time exercises, but principles to be incorporated into the fabric of your everyday life. It's this consistency that will enable a shift, guiding you towards a more harmonious and prosperous future.

The journey towards a harmonious and abundant life doesn't mean that you'll never experience disappointment or pain. Life will continually present challenges and lessons. Instead, it's about cultivating an inner resilience, using your heart-wisdom and mindful practices to navigate life's storms with grace, while consistently anchoring yourself in peace, love, and gratitude.

Remember, you aren't alone in this journey. Connect with others who resonate with your pursuits, creating a supportive and positive tribe. Surround yourself with those who uplift you and respect your journey. Engage in nourishing and fulfilling relationships that feed your soul and encourage your growth.

A harmonious and abundant future is no fairy-tale. It's attainable and lies just a decision away: the decision to comprehend and adopt a holistic, integrated approach towards life, balancing heart and mind, logic and intuition, shadow work and gratitude, self-care and service. It's making small, consistent steps towards the life you envision for yourself.

As we part ways at this stage, remember that your journey isn't a solo endeavor. You are part of the beautiful, interconnected web of life. Your vibrational shifts and spiritual growth don't just uplift you, but also those around you. Your personal journey towards harmony and abundance is, in essence, a gift to the world.

Finally, trust in your journey. Differences from others aren't anomalous but highlight your uniqueness. Validate your path, tune into your heart's wisdom, and know that an exciting, harmonious, and abundant future awaits you. So, be gentle with yourself as you move forward. All will unfold in its perfect timing and in alignment with your highest good.

We may have reached the end of this book, but your journey continues. Carry these lessons forward as you navigate toward a harmonious and abundant future, stepping into the limitless potential of your truth. May the road ahead be one of joy, love, growth, and fulfillment. And always remember, dear friend, the greatest journey is within.